fresh

For anyone who wants to ensure that they start their university experience well – and finish even better
Matt Summerfield

Accessible, daily bite-size chunks of Christian wisdom
David Jackman

Health warning: this book may permanently change your life!!
Jonathan Oloyede

A funny, realistic and practical guide to life as a Christian and as a student
Joel Edwards

A great read in preparation for going to university as a Christian student. An essential read once you arrive!
Stephen Gaukroger

If you think Jesus and the Bible are irrelevant, try this lively and challenging book. It could change your life . . .
David Wenham

Krish Kandiah

fresh

Bite-sized inspiration
for new students

ivp

INTER-VARSITY PRESS
Norton Street, Nottingham NG7 3HR, England
Email: ivp@ivpbooks.com
Website: www.ivpbooks.com

First published 2008

British Library Cataloguing in Publication Data
A catalogue record for this book is available from the British Library.

ISBN: 978-1-84474-275-2

Set in 10/12.5pt Myriad
Typeset in Great Britain by CRB Associates, Reepham Norfolk
Printed in Great Britain by Ashford Colour Press Ltd., Gosport, Hampshire.

Inter-Varsity Press publishes Christian books that are true to the Bible and that communicate the gospel, develop discipleship and strengthen the church for its mission in the world.

Inter-Varsity Press is closely linked with the Universities and Colleges Christian Fellowship, a student movement connecting Christian Unions in universities and colleges throughout Great Britain, and a member movement of the International Fellowship of Evangelical Students. Website: www.uccf.org.uk

THANK YOU

Mum and Dad for supporting me through university, for food packages, washing and patience . . .

Nigel, Kim, Rod and Daryl for mentoring me as a student . . .

Jenny for introducing me to UCCF . . .

Andy, Adrian and Jeremy for being my Daniel, Meschach and Shadrach . . .

BSKSh (Albanian IFES movement) for teaching me about student life in another culture . . .

Naomi, Steph and Joshua for offering a student perspective on the manuscript . . .

Dave, Peter, Jo and David for providing expert input from decades of student ministry . . .

IVP whose books continue to help me and whose staff encouraged me to compile these pages . . .

Eleanor, Alison, Daryl and Sally who have helped shape the book . . .

Ash, Chris, Libby, and Paddy for road testing ideas . . .

But most of all to Miriam for making this book project possible, for honing the manuscript, for working through every syllable on numerous occasions, for ideas and vision. You are the best . . .

FEELING REALLY EXCITED STUDYING HISTORY?

FREQUENTLY REALIZING EVERYTHING SEEMS HOPELESS?

FRIENDLY RELATIONSHIPS ENERGIZING SINGLE HETEROSEXUAL?

A levels: check. UCAS form: check. Required grades: check. Childhood: check. Time to collect together overdraft, laptop, railcard, iPod, pot plant. Time to go it alone with cooking, dating, studying. Time to take faith out of its comfort zone and into Freshers Week.

Fresh provides daily inspiration for new students, covering everything from writing essays to writing home, from making friends to making the grade, from debt to dating. *Fresh* offers a challenging introduction to maintaining a strong personal Christian faith but keeps its main emphasis on discovering how Christian students can make the most of their faith, relationships and studies.

FOR READING EXPLANATION START HERE . . .

Fresh is designed for those who are filled with excitement at the prospect of university life, and those who are filled with anxiety. It is for those who are unsure whether or not to stick with Christianity at university, and for those who are determined to put God first in the years ahead.

Fresh is designed to be read one chapter per day during those first 35 days of university life. Each week looks at a major area of student life. (Not that these areas are easily separated out. In fact we will learn better how to integrate our faith with our whole university experience.)

Each week starts with a range of challenges to help us step out in faith and put the material into practice. It will also be possible to see how other Christian students are experiencing their first few weeks, so log on to www.freshspace.org to find out more and access extra material. Many university Christian unions may well be using this book to set the programme for the first five weeks of term, so look out for their meetings and join a small group to discuss the issues with other freshers.

CONTENTS

WEEK 1: FAITH

UNIVERSITY CHALLENGE: WEEK 1

EXPRESSO CHALLENGE

Plot a graph of your personal growth in faith.

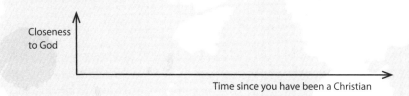

Which were the times in your life that you were closest to God and why?

EXTREME CHALLENGE

Aim to spend time in personal prayer and Bible reading each day for the
entire academic year
OR
Aim to pray weekly with a friend

EXPRESSION CHALLENGE

Draw or paint an image that expresses your relationship
with God. Take a digital photo of the image and
share it online at www.freshspace.org.

CHOICE

I had an identity makeover before I left for university. I binned the knitted tanktops and invested in new jeans and trainers. I upgraded my music system and updated my CD collection. I got a haircut, a kettle and a brand new duvet cover.

Anyone visiting me in my room that first week would have discovered I was a big fan of U2 (large poster on wall), majoring in chemistry (massive tome on shelf) and planning to live on curry (array of spices in cupboard). But was my Bible going to be kept in the drawer or on the shelf? This was more than a practical dilemma. It was a faith crisis. Was I going to be a secret Christian or a serious Christian?

The decision-making process of whether or not to commit to God was similar to the way I chose my university in the first place. It involved mind, heart and will.

MIND

Open days. Prospectuses. Interviews. Once we have decided which subject we want to pursue from the thousands on offer, we then try to find a university that actually offers the course. We research what the course involves, and what grades are needed.

When we commit to following Jesus, we need to do some research to be sure that he really existed, that he was who he claimed to be, that he actually died on the cross and that he really came back from the dead. We need to find out what he offers and what following him costs.

HEART

I looked round one university in a storm and another on a beautiful summer's day. Guess which one I preferred? We can't base our choice solely on a sudden rush of emotion, but feelings are certainly involved.

There are certain things we will feel if we are Christians. If we have never felt guilty about our sin and rebellion against God, if we never feel grateful for what Christ has done for us, if there is no sense of joy or wonder at God's grace, then we should consider whether our relationship with God is real or not.

WILL

Finally it's make-our-mind-up time and we have to sign the UCAS form. We are not signing whether we believe the universities of choice feel right or actually exist, but that we have every intention of going to study there. It is a decision of the will that affects our approach to A levels, our first years away from home, and probably our career and life journey.

The decision to commit to Jesus Christ is not only about what we know or what we believe – it is about what we do. It is a decision that will affect every aspect of our lives forever. Jesus wanted to make sure we didn't miss the point when he told the parable of two builders:

Therefore everyone who hears these words of mine and puts them into practice is like a wise man who built his house on the rock. The rain came down, the streams rose, and the winds blew and beat against that house; yet it did not fall, because it had its foundation on the rock. But everyone who hears these words of mine and does not put them into practice is like a foolish man who built his house on sand. The rain came down, the steams rose, and the winds blew and beat against that house, and it fell with a great crash. (Matthew 7:24–27)

Imagine two people sitting in the same church building on the same Sunday morning. They both hear the same sermon. They both wear WWJD wrist bands and display a fish sticker on their car. They both shake the pastor's hand on the way out. For all the world knows there is no external difference between them. But one lets the words drift in one ear and out the other. The other puts a plan into action.

These two listeners are like the two men that build apparently identical houses. It is not until the storms come that the structural integrity of the houses is tested. The house which has a foundation dug into hard bedock withstands the pressure; the one built on sandy soil suffers severe subsidence!

Jesus is asking us to check beyond the external observation of religious rituals. He wants us to check if we are connecting head knowledge and heartfelt emotion to action.

Coming to university can reveal what our faith is really made of. Is it based on a real foundation connected to the bedrock of a personal relationship with Jesus? Or is it simply a house of cards that will fall down with the wind of change or the whiff of persecution?

Before my first chemistry lab session, I was shown a safety film. I saw contact lenses melting onto somebody's eyeballs. I saw girls whose long hair caught fire. I saw acids eating some poor student's hands. It was shocking. It was also quite different from the film they showed me when I applied for the course: students strolling around campus, laughing as they turned on Bunsen burners, and celebrating as they were handed first-class honours degrees!

The lecturers needed to ram home the message that we were being treated as adults and trusted with toxins, powerful acids and highly dangerous machinery. I had thought that the only way to die at university was out of boredom, but the film showed that the life of a chemistry undergraduate was hazardous.

Christianity is not a hobby we do for fun in our spare time. Our response to the Christian faith has life-or-death consequences. If we choose to check our foundations and put Jesus' words into practice, we choose a life that will weather the storms of university and beyond. If we just go with the flow, and allow God's word to impact only our ears and not our lives, then Jesus warns us that we can lose everything.

Some people decide to leave their faith at home when they go to university. Others decide to go with the flow, and over time drift away. Some decide to be secret Christians, others social Christians. Some people decide that their fresh start away from home will be made with Jesus clearly leading the way.

Which will you choose? The following chapters will help as you decide which course to take: not which academic course, but which faith course – hearing Jesus' words and living your own life, or hearing Jesus words and letting *him* lead the way.

COMMITMENT

I believe that Adolf Hitler was born in 1889. I believe he took his life in a bunker on 30 April 1945. I believe that between those two dates he was responsible for murdering around six million Jews. I believe many other things about Hitler, but I am not in any way, shape or form, a Nazi. To believe facts about someone is very different from trusting and following them.

What does it mean to be a Christian? It must mean more than believing certain facts about Jesus. Faith, as we have seen, combines intellectual assent, an emotional response and a personal trust in Jesus. Faith also involves both hearing Jesus' message and living it out. Christians call this message the gospel or good news.

The gospel is more than a bunch of bullet points to be memorized. The first biographies of Jesus tell us details of how he spent time with children, outcasts, religious experts, friends and family. They tell us the stories Jesus told, the emotions he felt, the conversations he had. The entire life and person of Jesus is the good news. However, right at the beginning of Mark's biography of Jesus, we get close to Jesus' own summary of the absolute basics of the gospel message.

Jesus went into Galilee proclaiming the good news of God. 'The time has come,' he said. 'The kingdom of God is near. Repent and believe the good news!' (Mark 1:14–15)

'THE TIME HAS COME'

Jesus declares that he is the turning point of human history. The decisive moment the Jewish people have been waiting for has arrived because Jesus has turned up. Now the calendar has to be reset. God himself has stepped into history.

'THE KINGDOM OF GOD IS NEAR'

All of history has been a preparation for this moment when the kingly reign of God would arrive in a new way. Looking around at our world, we can see that things are not as they ought to be. The world is not as God designed it or desires it to be. It is full of disaster, disease and death, and all this damage is because we abuse God's gift of free will when we choose to ignore him and his words. But Jesus promises that God's perfect reign over the earth is on its way. Jesus embodies this promise as he rules over disaster, calming a storm (Mark 4:35–41); as he rules over demons (Mark 5:1–20); as he rules over disease, healing a woman with a haemorrhage (Mark 5:25–34); and as he rules over death, raising Jairus' daughter to life (Mark 5:35–43). Jesus is the King and he brings with him a taste of the future coming of God's kingdom, and a taste of the justice, compassion, life and joy of the coming reign of God.

'REPENT'

Every time we disobey God in thought, word or action, it is an act of rebellion against his rightful rule over his universe and should be punished. The fitting punishment for this treason is death. In the light of this, the good news that God's rule is coming might look like bad news. But Jesus offers us a time of amnesty. Now is the time to make peace with God, asking him for forgiveness. This amnesty is only possible because of what Jesus did on the cross.

It was on the cross that Jesus offered himself to receive God the Father's punishment in our place. The obedient Son offered himself as a sacrifice so that our rebellion could be forgiven. The cross of Jesus calls us to repent, turning away from a rebellious lifestyle, deciding to live under the rule of God, and living lives modelled on Jesus' self-sacrificial servanthood (Mark 10:45).

'BELIEVE THE GOOD NEWS'

Jesus therefore offers good news. It was good news for first-century Jews living under the oppression of Roman occupation. It is good news for us living in a spendthrift, selfish, sex-mad society. Good news because Jesus' resurrection proves that his sacrifice was accepted. Good news because our small sacrifices for the sake of Christ will be shown to be worthwhile. Good news because our decisions about every area of life – who we date, how we study, where we shop, what we invest our lives into, why we are concerned about the environment – will show into eternity who we have pledged allegiance to.

Getting to know Jesus, what he stood for, who he is, and what he has done for us is life-changing stuff. It stands at the heart of what we believe. Being a Christian means repenting, believing the good news and committing to following Jesus. Take a look at the prayer below. If you have never said words like these to God, then take some time out to seriously consider this commitment. If you know that you have committed your life to following Jesus in the past, take a few moments to check that this prayer still reflects where your heart is with God.

Prayer of commitment

Father God, thank you that Jesus came into the world to live and die for me. I am so sorry for thinking I was my own master and ignoring and disobeying you for so long. I recognize that I ought to be punished too. Please forgive me for my sins because of what Jesus did on the cross in my place. I want you to be King of my life and I offer you all of me. Please help me to live for you every day with the help of the Holy Spirit. Amen.

Student phone deals often look too good to be true. Some seem to offer more free minutes a month than there are actual minutes. Some handsets they appear to throw in would have Jack Bauer leaving the counter-terrorism unit in favour of pursuing higher education. It might seem the phone to die for – until you read the fine print. You need a scanning electron microscope to find it, but there it tells you that you will be locked into this contract until your grandchildren come along and that after three weeks your package is downgraded so you won't actually be able to make any calls at all!

Becoming a Christian may at first sight seem to be one of those too-good-to-be-true deals. It offers forgiveness from God, a fresh start and freedom from guilt in this life, and eternal happiness in the next. **But the Bible is very clear and upfront about the fact that following Jesus is both completely free and utterly costly.** The cross of Christ is the place where this apparent paradox is most clearly seen. The logic of the cross is set out in Peter's first letter.

But if you suffer for doing good and you endure it, this is commendable before God. To this you were called, because Christ suffered for you, leaving you an example, that you should follow in his steps. 'He committed no sin, and no deceit was found in his mouth.' When they hurled their insults at him,

he did not retaliate; when he suffered, he made no threats. Instead, he entrusted himself to him who judges justly. He himself bore our sins in his body on the cross, so that we might die to sins and live for righteousness; 'by his wounds you have been healed'. For 'you were like sheep going astray', but now you have returned to the Shepherd and Overseer of your souls.
(1 Peter 2:20–25)

Peter was writing to Christian slaves scattered throughout northern Turkey who were experiencing all sorts of abuse because of their commitment to Christ. Peter does not tell them that their experience is unusual. He does not tell them that everything will be okay. Instead Peter tells them that suffering for God is part and parcel of the calling to be a Christian and the cost of following Christ.

The cross teaches us that following Jesus means walking in his footsteps. Those footsteps took Jesus to pain and persecution. They took him through distress and death. When we are experiencing difficulties in our Christian life we are called to emulate Jesus' powerful trust in God the Father and not seek revenge or retaliation. The German resistance leader, theologian and martyr Dietrich Bonhoeffer put it like this: 'When Christ calls a man, he bids him come and die.'[1] Peter makes it clear that the cross of Christ is to be the model for our lifestyle. Jesus left us in no doubt that to be a Christian is to 'take up' your cross and follow him (Mark 8:34). The cross shows us that following Jesus is incredibly costly.

If the cross was only an example for us we would be in serious trouble. It would make our acceptance with God dependent on how well we have lived or how much suffering we have experienced. But Peter also makes crystal clear the fact that the cross reconciles us with God as a free gift (verse 24). We are forgiven because Christ willingly took our sins upon himself. When he died, God poured all his anger for the sins of the world on his Son; by so doing Christ's death satisfied God's perfectly just anger at our sin. This is such a powerful idea that the whole of Scripture resounds with it. Peter's words echo those of Isaiah: 'We all, like sheep, have gone astray, each of us has turned to our own way; and the Lord has laid on him the iniquity of us all' (Isaiah 53:6). The cross shows us that life for the Christian is a free gift at Christ's expense.

The cross is the key to our Christian life, showing us Christ as our Saviour and substitute. This fact motivates us to live lives of grateful thanks for God's gracious mercy. It empowers our worship. It defines our identity. It ignites our passion for God.

The cross is the guide to our Christian life, showing us Christ as our model and master. This motivates us to stand up for Christ no matter what abuse we get. It inspires us to serve him whatever the cost. It enables us to keep going in our master's footsteps when the going gets tough.

It is advisable to check the hidden cost of too-good-to-be-true phone deals. It is wise to consider carefully the clearly-stated cost of following Christ. Jesus offers us the free gift of forgiveness paid for at great personal expense. He offers us a costly life of following a crucified Saviour. It's not too good to be true – it's too good to miss.

CONFIDENCE

Dr Cox was the scariest member of the chemistry faculty. His tutorials were infamous. He could reduce students to tears by showing them up in front of their peers. His labs were long and laborious. One night I was the last person to leave. As usual my experiment had gone horribly wrong and I had to stay behind to clean up all the glassware. I felt his cold breath behind me as he said with disdain, 'So Kandiah, I hear you are one of those Christians.'

I felt my brain freeze. Dr Cox went on to explain why he thought faith was intellectual suicide. I didn't know what to say. I carried on washing my test tubes and went home feeling like I'd let the side down.

Like many, Dr Cox saw faith as the ability to believe what we know isn't true. Even many Christians describe faith as a blind leap. Or at least, what takes us the rest of the way when facts only get us 51% of the way there. But faith is more than wishful thinking. Jesus said:

Don't you believe that I am in the Father, and that the Father is in me? The words I say to you I do not speak on my own authority. Rather, it is the Father, living in me, who is doing his work. Believe me when I say that I am in the Father and the Father is in me; or at least believe on the evidence of the miracles themselves. (John 14:10–12)

Philip had just heard Jesus claim to be 'the way, the truth and the life'. But Philip struggles to believe this. So he asks Jesus to show him God the Father. Jesus' words patiently address our impatience. He does not tell Philip and the other disciples to close their eyes and psyche themselves up, or just blindly accept what they can't see.

Imagine we took this approach to crossing the road. Standing at the kerb we can never be totally certain that we will make it to the other side. A heavy object may fall out of the sky, or there may be superglue on the road, or James Bond's invisible car may run us over. But this lack of certainty does not mean that we put our fingers in our ears, close our eyes, scream and make a dash for it. Instead we gather a reasonable amount of evidence based on what our senses tell us, and what we know from experience, and then take our lives in our hands and step out in faith.

Jesus asks his disciples to open their eyes, use their minds and reflect on what they had heard him say and seen him do, and then make an informed decision to follow him in faith. This approach to believing in God is a far cry from intellectual suicide.

As Christians, we are called to love God with our hearts, souls and minds. We sometimes forget the last bit, but turning our brains off is not an option. Christianity is real because it is true. There is plenty of evidence that it is not just 'true for you', but genuinely, universally, and authentically true.

I believe that Christianity is true and our faith is well-founded for three different reasons:

EVIDENCE

The Christian faith makes the confident assertion that when the Bible claims something happened it really did take place. For example, there is excellent historical evidence that Jesus really lived, died and rose again (see the website www.freshspace.org for some helpful books).

EXPERIENCE

Many of us can testify that we have experienced the presence of God in worship. We have seen God answer our prayers. We have watched him change our lives and the lives of others we know.

EXPLANATION

The Christian faith offers the best explanation of the facts of human existence. It provides a reason for morality, hope, purpose, beauty, and relationships. When people wonder what on earth they are here for, or why they feel scared about death, or angry about injustice, the Christian faith offers coherent and compelling answers.

I wish I had understood this when challenged by Dr Cox. I wish I had asked him with love and respect how he dealt with the compelling evidence for Christ, how his answers to the big questions in life compared to the coherent explanations of Christianity. I wish I had found out what he made of the consistent experiences Christians have of God in their lives.

I wish I could have shown him that the Christian faith is not a matter of intellectual suicide, but intellectual pride. This is not an arrogant, boastful pride, but a confidence in the credibility of Christianity and the reality of the living God.

> **Try the following:**
>
> www.bethinking.org
> www.rejesus.com
> www.cis.org.uk/resources.shtml

CORE

When I was 18, I thought Christians were either charismatics or Salvationists. I thought all Christians either marched around town with the Salvation Army brass band or fell over in the Spirit. Suddenly, on arriving at university I met people from all sorts of churches. I was overwhelmed as I realized that what mattered most was not which denomination people were from, but whether they loved and followed God.

Then I met the campus chaplain. He didn't believe that Jesus had lived, died or risen from the dead. It didn't stop him joining in the worship – he said it was an inspiring story. Then I met my flatmate who said that as a Christian and a Mormon, she believed the angel Moroni had revealed himself only to the Church of the Latter Day Saints.

The title 'Christian' seemed to be covering a lot of bases, from 'the last time I went to church was when I was christened as a baby' to 'I am a member of a cult group from the USA' to 'I believe Christ is a myth, but an interesting myth . . . '

It was not much different in Jesus' day. There was a whole range of Jewish groups, all claiming to represent God. There were Sadducees, Zealots and Essenes, all with their own particular take on the Jewish faith. The most infamous group were the Pharisees. They had two problems. First, they had a wonderful public image as morally upstanding people, yet were blatantly motivated by power and status. Second, they saw Jesus' miracles and heard his teaching and yet decided that he was a blasphemous traitor who deserved the death penalty. Both their lives and their doctrines were in error.

Paul echoes this when he writes to a young church leader:

Watch your life and doctrine closely. Persevere in them, because if do, you will save both yourself and your hearers. (1 Timothy 4:16)

Often we feel happier emphasizing either our lifestyle or our beliefs. Some Christians are so focused on the doctrines of truth that they can appear as though they are on a heresy hunt twenty-four hours a day and their attitude falls short of Jesus' loving compassion. Other Christians work really hard at watching their outward lives, but they have a shaky understanding of what the Christian faith really is.

In the following chapters we will be focusing mainly on watching our lives at university, but we need to make doubly sure that this is always balanced by watching our doctrine carefully too. Doubly, because Paul says that this can save both ourselves and others.

There's not much difference between the chemical composition of sodium chloride (NaCl) and sodium cyanide (NaCN). Both are similar white powders. One we sprinkle sparingly on our chips, but using the same amount of the other could wipe out a whole queue of hungry customers. A few minor differences and something tasty becomes something deadly.

We need to be careful what we put on our chips, but we need to be more careful what we believe. We need to feed on the truth, not poison ourselves or others. We need to be clear about the essentials of the faith.

Once there was a lot at stake for anyone daring to call themselves a Christian: martyrdom at the (literal) stake perhaps, or persecution from empire, friends and family. No surprise then that people did not claim to be Christians lightly. It is a very different world we live in now, at least in the UK. Many are Christians because of family tradition, and many claim to be Christian, yet hold a variety of views.

Using the term 'evangelical' has become a way to distinguish between those who call themselves Christians, and those who actually believe certain core truths of the gospel. The term cuts across denominational boundaries and focuses on the central doctrines of the Christian faith, such as the authority of the Bible, God as Trinity, Jesus' death and resurrection. Evangelicals can agree to disagree on other matters like the age of the earth, baptism (when and how), charismatic gifts or the role of women in the church, recognizing that there are true followers on both sides of these debates.

Christian unions are often very good at distinguishing between these essential and non-negotiable core beliefs and secondary issues. CUs can include Christians who speak in tongues and Christians who believe the gifts of the Holy Spirit ended with the apostles; people who believe that the world was created in six literal days and those who believe in evolution over a six-billion-year period. By agreeing on the essential issues of the gospel, we can avoid fistfights and fallouts over these other non-essential issues.

The university chaplain and the girl on my corridor could not agree on these evangelical essentials. To my understanding, they were not saved and I needed to lovingly witness to them as much as to my atheistic lecturer or my agnostic friends.

Once we learn how to distinguish between primary and secondary issues we can learn from one another and serve God together as a united body on campus, demonstrating our unity based on grace and truth.

> In essentials, unity. In non-essentials, liberty.
> In all things, love.
> (attributed to Augustine of Hippo)

CONVINCED?

Way back in the last century, before e-mail, mobiles and sms, I had a girlfriend who took a year out in Germany. In order to communicate we had to prearrange the time and place. One cold, dark winter's night, I expected her to be at the phone box by a tram stop north of Cologne at 11 pm. I dialled confidently, but no one answered. I waited a few minutes and tried again. After five attempts I began to wonder. Where was she? Had she fallen for someone closer to hand? Had I been dumped? I thought our love was strong, but suddenly she was five minutes late and I was plagued with doubt.

Doubt is something that affects all relationships. It is painful, uncomfortable and catches us unawares. At the same time it is normal, healthy and to be expected. We see this paradox often in the Bible, where godly men and women struggle to keep trusting. Mark's Gospel shows the conflict in the prayer of a father anxious for his son's life: 'I do believe, help me overcome my unbelief!' (Mark 9:24).

The Psalms are also full of weird and wonderful prayers. Weird because we would get some strange looks if we dared to pray them today at a public prayer meeting. Wonderful because they show us the authentic sort of relationship God wants from us. He doesn't want us just to say what we think we ought to say. God wants to see honesty and integrity.

Psalm 73 is a journey through doubt. The Psalmist feels as if he is walking the knife edge between faith and unbelief and his feet are slipping beneath him (verse 2). Without a doubt, doubt is unsettling: Are we . . . ? Aren't we . . . ? Is God . . . ? Isn't God . . . ? The foundations of our life are at stake. It's certainly not a place where we want to be for long.

The Psalmist's doubt doesn't arise because of a trauma, a loss or a betrayal. It comes from a reaction common to many Christians at university. As he looked around he saw unbelievers having fun, without a care for God's rules. He was jealous of their lifestyle and it made him question his own moral stance: 'Surely in vain I have kept my heart pure . . . ' (verse 13).

We may envy the lifestyles of the rich and famous in *Hello* magazine. Or we may watch our housemates and course-mates making the most of their freedom and question whether our faith is worth the hassle.

We learn from this psalm that honesty in expressing frustration does not make us spiritual losers. We learn that nobody, however mature or famous, is immunized against an attack of doubt.

But the psalm does not end here. Verse 17 tells us that as the doubter did what he normally did and went to worship God in the temple, things began to make sense. Many of us fear that Christian routines are unhealthy as they can make our worship of God cold and stuck in a rut. But this psalm shows us that the regular disciplines of the Christian faith can help us when we are struggling. Keeping up regular church and CU attendance, prayer times and Bible studies, can put us in places where God can speak and reassure us. It can put us in places where Christian friends can encourage or challenge us.

When the Psalmist felt that his feet were slipping, God's response was to show him the slippery ground non-believers are on (verse 18). He saw the eternal perspective. Their pleasure is short-lived. Their security does not count in the long run. When faced with the choice to give up on his faith, he saw that the alternative was even more unsettling.

The instant gratification of life lived without God is worthless compared to the treasure of eternal life with God. 'Yet I am always with you; you hold me by my right hand, you guide me . . . and afterwards you will take me into glory. Whom have I in heaven but you? . . . earth has nothing I desire besides you' (verses 23–25).

Doubt is a strange thing. It can only exist where there is faith in the first place. **Doubt can turn our faith into unbelief or it can turn it into a deeper trust in God. So doubt is not the opposite of faith or the end of faith, but rather a proof of faith.**

The Psalmist offers a doubt-busting strategy:

1. Confide in God.
2. Carry on Christian disciplines.
3. Consider God's perspective and feelings.
4. Compare the alternatives.
5. Counteract the doubts.

On that cold winter's night back in the last century, I counteracted my doubts by remembering what I knew for certain about my girlfriend. She was dependable, reliable, trustworthy and faithful. She had proved it to me before. Over the years our trust grew despite my nagging doubts. Eventually she even married me!

I get just as paranoid in my relationship with God. When bad things happen in my life. When God seems to ignore my prayers. When I fail God over and over again. When I can't answer all the questions. When I wish I could be someone else for a short time. When I am just not convinced. I am well practised now at counteracting doubts by bringing to mind all the things I know for certain. Usually this centres around the cross of Jesus which never fails to ram home God's love, grace and faithfulness. Even in the darkest moment of history, God was doing something for us almost beyond belief. Surely God is good to us (verse 1).

Surely God is good to Israel,
*   to those who are pure in heart.*
But as for me, my feet had almost slipped;
*   I had nearly lost my foothold.*
For I envied the arrogant
*   when I saw the prosperity of the wicked . . .*
Surely in vain have I kept my heart pure;
*   in vain have I washed my hands in innocence.*
All day long I have been afflicted;
*   and every morning brings new punishments . . .*
When I tried to understand all this,
*   it troubled me deeply*
till I entered the sanctuary of God;
*   then I understood their final destiny.*
Surely you place them on slippery ground;
*   you cast them down to ruin . . .*
Whom have I in heaven but you?
*   And earth has nothing I desire besides you.*
My flesh and my heart may fail,
*   but God is the strength of my heart*
*   and my portion forever.*
Those who are far from you will perish;
*   you destroy all who are unfaithful to you.*
But as for me, it is good to be near God.
*   I have made the Sovereign Lord my refuge;*
*   I will tell of all your deeds.*
(Psalm 73:1–3, 13–14, 16–18, 25–28)

CHALLENGE

I recently had to say goodbye to my precious Apple Macbook Pro. It was a fond farewell. After all it had become a close friend. It had accompanied me to several continents. It had been with me during some tough times. I had taken great care of it – I'd defragged its hard drive, wiped the monitor clean, kept it charged up and stroked its brushed aluminium case regularly. I'd bought it a protective bag. I had hardly let it out of my sight. It even came to bed with me sometimes. But my job had ended and I had to give it back.

As I handed it over I remembered Jesus' words: *'What good will it be for you to gain the whole world, yet forfeit your soul?' (Matthew 16:26).*

Jesus tells us that our soul is the most precious thing we have. If we exchanged it for Bill Gates's fortune or the combined wealth of the West we would be short-changed. When we reflect on the king's ransom that was paid for our eternal life with God, we should value our spiritual life more than we do.

Many of us consider reconciliation with God to be something that we deserve rather than an incredibly costly gift of grace. God deems our souls to be worth the creation of the entire universe, worth a rescue plan that took thousands of years to complete and, most importantly, worth the sacrifice of the life of his only Son. How far do we go? Do we invest as much time and effort in taking care of our souls as we do in taking care of our other prized possessions?

Jesus tells us that even our body parts are disposable compared to our spiritual life.

If your eye causes you to stumble, pluck it out. It is better to enter the kingdom of heaven with one eye than to have two eyes and be thrown into hell. (Mark 9:47)

Jesus is not promoting self-mutilation or DIY eye surgery. He is telling us that we must be prepared to do whatever it takes, whatever the cost, to hold on to our integrity as Christians. Take radical action to live for God, to love and serve only him.

We are good at investing time into caring for our bodies through diet and exercise and fashion. We make sure we are caring for our minds through study, stimulation and relaxation. But some of us have a laid back approach to spiritual growth, as if it will just happen naturally as we grow older.

My daughter was four when the stabilizers came off her bike. She could ride well before so she was very disconcerted to find that she had to relearn the same skill while keeping her balance. When we go to university, our spiritual stabilizers are removed: home church, family and youth leaders are left behind. It is natural to wobble a bit in our faith.

My daughter soon learned that the harder she pedalled the longer she would keep moving; that if she stopped, she would fall off. And that hurt. The Apostle Paul had a similar sense of momentum and intentionality about his own spiritual growth. He writes 'I press on towards the goal . . .' (Philippians 3:14). He knew that to keep going as a Christian, he had to keep pedalling. He often used metaphors of endurance to describe his spiritual journey: 'I have fought the good fight, . . . finished the race, . . . kept the faith' (2 Timothy 4:7).

Paul's secret was that he never stopped going forward in his Christian development. Christians are like young cyclists – we need to keep on going and keep on growing in order to stay alive spiritually.

The rest of this book provides many tips how to do this, exploring practical, biblical and devotional angles on living for God at university. But first, here are ten practical ideas on how to begin to care for our souls, our most valuable possession.

1. **Pray:** A relationship with God will only develop if we spend time with him on a daily basis.
2. **Read the Bible:** Scripture is spiritual food to nourish our souls. Find time and space in the day to read God's word.
3. **Be accountable:** Ask someone you respect to check up on how you are doing.
4. **Join a local church:** Worship God and be with his family.
5. **Connect with the Christian Union:** This exists to help Christians support each other and live for Christ while at university.
6. **Go public:** Let people know that you are a Christian.
7. **Integrate:** Resist dividing life into the spiritual and the non-spiritual. Learn how faith is involved in every part of life.
8. **Integrity:** Recognize the pressures of living away from home in a morally challenging environment and decide on some principles regarding alcohol, sex, money and time.
9. **Balance:** Resist spending all your time in Christian meetings or with your non-Christian friends.
10. **Give:** Practice giving, even on a small budget, to demonstrate God's grace and to establish lifelong habits of sacrificial generosity.

WEEK 2: RELATIONSHIPS

Day 1. God
Day 2. friends
Day 3. parents
Day 4. boy/girlfriend
Day 5. church
Day 6. Christian Union
Day 7. university

UNIVERSITY CHALLENGE: WEEK 2

EXPRESSO CHALLENGE
Send this postcard to a Christian friend at your home church (you may wish to use an envelope!):

Dear...

Please would you help me to be accountable at university in the following areas:

Please would you pray about:

I am really excited about:

Thank you very much.

EXTREME CHALLENGE

Send some thank you texts to encourage friends from the following categories:

(a) church
(b) family
(c) friends
(d) old school/college

EXPRESSION CHALLENGE

Write two Haiku poems about university relationships following the scanning of the example below. Share them at www.freshspace.org.

Japanese poem
with seventeen syllables
only three lines long.

It was a match made in heaven. God decided that we were to exist. He made us in his image to demonstrate his character. He made us free to rebel against him, knowing that his own Son would have to die in our place, knowing that only some would accept his offer of reconciliation. God created us, not because he was lonely or bored or insecure, but because he wanted a relationship with us.

We were not born primarily for work, for fun or for success. We were born for relationship. Our relationship with each other and God is a mirror of the three-way relationship of the Trinity: Father, Son and Holy Spirit. Amazingly, we are invited into that relationship, which is more intimate, and more selfless than we can ever imagine.

This divine-love relationship is to be the foundation of all our relationships. Get this right and we will begin to get a handle on all the other relationships. Jesus' key commandment for us is, **'Love the Lord your God with all your heart and with all your soul and with all your mind' (Matthew 22:37).**

HEART

The Psalms are full of heart language: 'I thirst for you, my whole being longs for you' (Psalm 63:1). As we have seen in the previous section, God expects us to relate to him honestly in times of joy, longing, anger, worry, guilt and gratitude.

God knows that our lives are a rollercoaster of emotions. We are easily swayed by changing circumstances as well as more trivial factors like the weather, how much sleep we've had, or what we've eaten. Although we are to relate to God with our emotions, our emotional state must not be allowed to determine our relationship with God. If we begin to fall into this trap, our relationship with God will become very changeable and insecure. When emotional engagement is weak, we can feel, and then act, as though God were not there.

SOUL

Our relationship with God must be spiritual, but our understanding of spiritual is often too vague. It conjures up images of monks and vows of silence. Jesus challenges this view by his life and teachings. His second key commandment follows immediately after his first: 'Love your neighbour as yourself' (Matthew 22:39). Jesus-like spirituality is not isolation but engagement.

The danger here is that we constantly whizz from one activity to another, never stopping long enough to think or pray. This is a big danger for students. We can be manically busy: trying to study, going to church, helping new Christians and influencing student politics. All of these are good things until they happen not out of, but at the expense of, a relationship with God. Our father-child bond with God can easily mutate into something more like an employer-employee contract.

MIND

Our intellects must be involved as we worship God in spirit and truth. We are supposed to get to know God through using our minds to discern truth from error.

But we must be wary of a cold rationalism, where we merely assent to the truth of God's existence in the same way that I assent to the truth of the melting point of iron being 1538 degrees centigrade. This fact has no emotional impact on me, nor any significance for my actions (unless I am imprisoned in iron chains and happen to have a super-hot blowtorch available).

Jesus' command to love God with heart, soul and mind challenges us to develop balance in our relationship with God, and work on all three aspects simultaneously. Anchoring our love in discerning the truth about him will prevent a rollercoaster ride of emotions. Relating to God honestly with our emotions will prevent us from becoming cold in our faith. Engaging our spiritual life with doing good works shows that our relationship with God is active and healthy.

But developing our relationship with God in all these ways avoiding all the pitfalls is a tall order. Where are we supposed to begin?

Many Christians throughout the centuries have found the daily discipline of setting aside a regular time to read the Bible and pray on their own or in a small group as fundamental to their faith. The danger of having 'quiet times', as they are often known, is that they can divide life into God-time and me-time. But the danger of not having this daily discipline is that our Bibles can be unopened for weeks at a time and our prayer life may dry up.

There are many creative ideas to keep a quiet time real. Here are some of my favourites:

Running with God: Plug in your iPod and listen to the Bible while you run (walk, jog, cycle or drive). Use landmarks to pray for different people, places and issues.

Writing to God: Use paper and pen to focus your mind by making notes on the Bible passage, expressing worship to God and keeping a prayer diary.

Breakfast with God: As soon as you wake up, pray and read a chapter of the Bible, perhaps following daily notes (www.freshspace.org).

Supper with God: Use as an alternative to, or in addition to, an early-morning devotional time. Reflect on the day, repenting of wrong actions and thanking God for his blessings.

Hunger for God: Sacrificing our daily soap opera, coffee shop outing or trip to the gym for a week carves out time to spend with God and shows him that he comes first.

FRIENDS

Beginning student life is eerily like entering the Big Brother house. Suddenly we are living in close community with a bunch of total strangers. We feel we are being watched twenty-four hours a day. Life in the outside world seems to stand still. People stay up late talking and gossiping. Romances blossom and break up.

In this environment, people will do almost anything to fit in. Dress, diet and dialect begin to synchronize. Faith is in a very fragile position, and many Christian students either allow it to fall by the wayside, or seek refuge, retreating to be alone in their rooms or with other Christians.

Refuge is one thing: we all need some time out and the support of other Christians. Retreat is another: Jesus calls us to be involved in the social life of the people around us. It is here we can be salt (Matthew 5:13).

Salt was the ice of Jesus' day, preserving meat from decay. We may think the environment is already pretty off, but the people around us need us to slow down the decay and make a difference.

Jesus also warned that salt that loses its saltiness is no use to anyone. Strictly speaking, salt can't lose its saltiness. Sodium chloride doesn't go off or go stale. But it can become mixed with impurities so that it doesn't taste salty anymore. It is possible that if we try too hard to fit in with the people around us, we can become diluted and compromised and cease to be distinctive.

So we are called to this difficult position of being in the world but not of the world. Jesus is our model in this. He did not camp out at the temple or spend all his time in the company of the religious. On the contrary, he was often criticized for spending too much time with the sinful people who needed him (Luke 15:1–3). Yet although Jesus spent time with the moral misfits and the local losers he maintained his holiness.

Christians tend towards two opposites at university. Some turn into student monks who fill their diaries with CU meetings, between which they wear CU hoodies and listen to worship music on their iPods. Others turn into student chameleons who blend so well into life on the corridor that they are virtually indistinguishable from anyone else. They saunter over towards the bar and subtly sidle into the back of the occasional CU meeting. Jesus' example calls us to connect with Christians yet also spend quality time with other friends. He calls us to be fully part of the social life on campus, yet fully honouring to God in all that we do.

This double-whammy of friendship-building can be especially intimidating for those of us who struggle to make even two friends, let alone two whole groups of friends. Loneliness is a common condition at uni for all sorts of people and all sorts of reasons. Despite being surrounded by peers, there is the isolation of being far away from the people who have known and loved us. This isolation is excruciatingly painful. God made us for relationships, yet in this broken world loneliness is rife. Even Jesus was misunderstood and misrepresented, ridiculed and rejected. Yet deciding to persevere and build even just two or three good friendships is a good goal.

The book of Daniel is a must-read for anyone going to university. Daniel and his compatriots Shadrach, Meshach and Abednego were forced to attend the University of Babylon to be trained in social sciences, government and politics. They decided to adapt to their environment to the extent that they wore the same kind of clothes, spoke the same language, and went to the same lectures. But they drew a line at eating the food. Whatever their reasons, the four of them were in it together. Their friendship survived several serious scrapes and their studying years; when they got their first graduate jobs they were still together, praying, watching out for one another, standing together for their God against all sorts of trouble.

This story inspired me when I was a student. I went to the CU to seek out some friends who would do the same for me. We met up once a week to chat honestly about the struggles we were facing, to read the Bible and to pray. This group was a real life-saver. My friends helped me combat temptations to compromise while the rest of my corridor was regularly getting drunk, high or laid. They helped keep me in check when CU meetings were eating up my time.

Many people look back at university life with great memories of being part of a 'Big Brother' type experience. Staying up late, chatting about music, films, God. Rallying around to support one another during tragedies. Finding any excuse for parties and celebrations. These sorts of things develop friendships that will last a lifetime.

Christian friendship needs to go at least one step further. Jesus loved to spend time with his close friends and with the crowds. But he also had a special concern for those on the margins of society. He touched the lepers, offered the cheats a fresh start, and refused to judge the prostitutes. **At university we have a specific responsibility to look out for the unloved, the outcast and the misfits.** Whether it's the international student with language difficulties, the guy next door with limited social skills or the mature student in the lecture theatre who always sits alone, we should keep our eyes open to find ways of demonstrating the gracious love of God.

PARENTS

As I watched mum and dad drive out of the car park I had mixed emotions. I was very glad to see them go. I was finally living independently. I had come of age! But then I had all those boxes to unpack by myself. And I was going to have to make my own dinner. And wash my own dishes afterwards! As the red tail lights disappeared into the distance I wondered if the tear I had spotted was one of sadness or possibly one of huge relief! I also wondered if my sister was plotting finally to get her hands on all my music and move into my room.

Going away to university is a big step. It signals a new stage of adulthood and independence. And with this come privileges and responsibilities. There are the privileges of deciding what we will eat and wear, how long we will sleep, and how much of our money we will spend. But there are also the responsibilities of taking care of our possessions, meeting deadlines, and playing our part as a fully adult, though long-distance, member of our family.

Leaving home is more than leaving our parents. Some of us leave behind younger siblings who assume a different role in the home, some a broken family, now with another empty space to deal with. We leave behind routines and traditions that have always been part and parcel of our identity. We miss out on regular get-togethers around the meal table or family gatherings with extended families. Some of us are pleased to escape parental control, but some will miss home like mad, and some will feel torn in two. And the emotions involved get overshadowed or forgotten by the intensity and pace of university life.

But they shouldn't.

He had just faced the worst week of his life. His so-called friends had abandoned him when he most needed them. He had been arrested and chained. He had been bombarded with false accusations, and when he had refused to speak, he had been tortured repeatedly. He knew that worse was to come and, although he was almost too weak to move, he had a cross tied to his back and was told to climb the stony path out of the city and up to the top of the hill.

But Jesus was not thinking about himself. He put up with this unjust humiliating pain because of the love he had for the helpless people around the world who would otherwise face God's wrath. And he was not only thinking about the millions whom he was saving, he was also thinking about his mother. At a time when anybody else would have been thinking only about themselves, Jesus asks his best friend John to take care of his mother when he is gone, and his mother to accept John as a son (John 19:26–27).

Jesus models the fact that even when we have every excuse to be self-absorbed, we have a responsibility to do right by our families. The Bible makes the point very clearly:

Anyone who does not provide for their relatives, and especially for their own household, has denied the faith and is worse than an unbeliever. (1 Timothy 5:8)

Being a Christian should make us better, not worse, sons or daughters. Here are five areas for considering how we can emulate Jesus in this area of our lives.

UNDERSTANDING

When babies feel hungry in the middle of the night, they scream until they get what they want, without any thought for their poor sleep-deprived carers. That consideration will develop as they grow up. Part of our responsibility in becoming independent is to be more sensitive to the needs of our family. Consider how they are feeling about our going away: the emotional wrench, the financial pressure, the hopes and fears, the empty nest, the challenges.

COMMUNICATION

When we worked abroad, one member of our student team would phone home less than once a month. He felt he had nothing to say to his parents. Another would have phoned every day if possible, still dependent on constant parental reassurance. Taking some initiative in regularly phoning or texting or visiting helps our family to know that we appreciate them and care about them.

RESPECT

Going home for the holidays can be difficult after the freedom of university. Most students experience culture shock. It is hard for a mum not to mother. My mum would happily still have bought my underwear, even after I had been married for ten years and had three children of my own! Be patient with your parents. Find ways to demonstrate that you honour them.

RESPONSIBILITY

Time to think about getting a TV licence for the first time. Time to put grandparents' birthdays in your diary. Time to think how to live on a budget without expecting to be bailed out if you don't manage. Time to be responsible.

PRAYER

It is hard to remember to pray for people we don't see every day. But praying regularly for our parents will help us gain a godly perspective on their welfare. Pray for their conversion, their problems at work, their everyday hassles. Many of our parents have prayed for us daily. Let's return the favour.

BOY/GIRLFRIEND

It is often assumed that university is where we will pair off and find our life mate. And this is true for many people. But it can be very difficult watching while everyone else finds their perfect match, wondering when our turn will come. It calls for a real trust in God when we don't meet Mr or Mrs Right in Freshers' week, or in our hall group, or in our entire time at uni.

But singles have no right to an inferiority complex. Jesus was single and lived the most fulfilled and perfect human life it is possible to live. Nor should singles get a superiority complex. I began university as part of a group of blokes who actually believed it was more spiritual to be single, based on a flawed understanding of 1 Corinthians 7. (I have since learned that marriage is not just for the weak who cannot control their sexual urges. It is part of God's original design for human life.)

So what about sex? Sex is good. Sex is fun. Sex was one of God's best ideas. Sex was part of God's plan even before things went wrong (Genesis 2:24–25).

Having a girlfriend or boyfriend at university comes hand in hand with the challenge of honouring God with our sexuality. Christians believe that sex is precious and should be saved for the safe environment of marriage. Choosing to abstain from sexual activity at university is a difficult principle to hold onto, especially with our friends spurring us on to be 'normal', and with the frequent time spent in and out of one another's bedrooms.

There are many good arguments for resisting temptation and waiting until marriage: sexual health issues, family planning issues, and sexual intimacy best expressed within the security of a 'forever whatever' relationship. But over and above all these reasons, God commands it (Hebrews 13:4). If we are dating, we should consider making a serious pledge of sexual abstinence and get some like-minded friends to hold us accountable.

An engaged couple decided to go on a holiday trip together. The sleeping arrangements were one double bed. They assured their church leader that they were not tempted at all sexually. Their pastor advised them to break off the engagement. He said that if they weren't tempted sexually in that scenario then there was something wrong with their relationship! Being accountable means helping to work out ways to spend time together, minimizing unnecessary temptations and discovering if the relationship has a future.

Deciding whether a relationship has a future is the vital question to ask in the common dilemma of Christians and non-Christians dating. The Bible teaches that believers are to marry believers (1 Corinthians 7:39). By implication we can extend this to dating. Dating someone we have no intention of marrying is asking for trouble or selfishly toying with another person's feelings. Dating a non-Christian will be very difficult if we are seeking to love God with our heart, soul and mind and put him first, as it will be very difficult to have a fulfilling intimate relationship with some-body who does not share that same goal or direction in their lives.

Imagine a Christian girl seeking to get closer to Christ. The Holy Spirit in her is working consistently and persistently to draw her to Christ. The non-Christian guy on the other hand is heading in the opposite direction. If she begins a romantic relationship, even with the initial desire to witness to him, she will face a tug either in her relationship with her boyfriend, or in her relationship with God, or in both of them. Somewhere along the line at least one of these relationships is going to be pulled apart. If she falls for a Christian guy, there is much more hope. As they are both drawn to Christ, they potentially grow closer to each other.

The Bible is full of love stories. Some have happy endings. Some have tragic endings. Enjoying a relationship with a boyfriend or girlfriend is a precious gift from God. And although common sense seems to fly out of the window when love is in the air, it is worth double-checking our principles with regard to our sexual purity, our impact on other friend-ships, our future together, and our worship of the God who invented relationships.

CHURCH

First week on campus and Al was a hot commodity! It was nice being wanted. He couldn't walk past the student union without managers, cuddly mascots and cashiers from a variety of banks all vying for his attention and his business. He wanted to join all of them! One offered him a free student railcard, another £50 cash, and another, HMV vouchers. He carefully weighed up which was the best offer, alongside which was most geographically convenient, which had the longest opening hours, and which had the coolest cards.

Whether it's banks, clubs and societies, or local churches, there is plenty of choice and plenty of enticement going on. But should we choose a church the same way we choose our bank? Do we just weigh up the same criteria: which is closest, which offers transport and lunches, or which service time allows us the longest lie-in?

Many Christian students look for a church just like their home church, or as different from it as possible! Many choose their church because it has great music or because it has great teaching. Apart from the fact that churches with both great worship and great teaching never seem to exist, we need to look closer at the other flaws in this approach.

The problem is that the emphasis is on what we can get out of church. Wanting our own spiritual needs to be met, wanting to feel comfortable worshipping God in a certain way, or wanting to hear our kind of teaching, is shopping for church in the same way that we choose a bank or a coffee shop.

Paul's illustration of the church as the body of Christ in 1 Corinthians 12:12–30 gives us the big picture of the incredible privilege of being part of it.

CHRIST LOVES THE CHURCH

Christ is the head of the body (Ephesians 1:22–23) and he loves the church (Ephesians 5:25). When the church is criticized or persecuted, it pains Jesus, who died for the church and will one day welcome her as his bride. If we love Jesus, we must love the whole body of the church.

WE ARE THE CHURCH BY DEFAULT

When we become Christians, we are filled with the Spirit of God and become part of the universal body of Christ (1 Corinthians 12:13). We cannot *go* to church because we *are* the church. But this does not mean we are exempt from meeting with our brothers and sisters. We are connected to the body and must not amputate ourselves from it. The motorbike courier with his icebox containing human organs demonstrates that body bits can exist outside a body, but not for long and not at their full potential (1 Corinthians 12:21–25).

WE NEED THE CHURCH AND THE CHURCH NEEDS US

A heart needs to receive blood and oxygen from the rest of the body. And the body needs the heart to circulate that blood and oxygen to the rest of the organs. God deliberately scattered his gifts throughout the church so that we would need one another. We need to be both receivers and givers. We need to receive the ministry of others but we also need to play our role (1 Corinthians 12:14–20).

Unity in diversity is the beauty and the witness of the church. God has made each of us different, and as we gather with people of different ages, life stages and life experiences, we see a taste of God's kingdom. God wants the church to be the one place on earth where polar opposites can come together. The CU can never do this as it will always be a gathering of students. There should never be a choice between church and CU attendance. It is both-and, not either-or. The church is rightly seen as our long-term permanent spiritual home, whereas CU is more like a short-term mission experience.

The decision to make church a priority is more important than choosing which local church to attend. However, as we saw in the last section, Jesus tells us to be discerning, so we do need to look for key signs that the congregation and its leaders are really trying to live out the gospel, worship God in spirit and truth and teach the Bible faithfully.

Some students spend their entire three years at university church-shopping. A better approach would be to do some web searching before leaving home and set a time limit for looking around. Why not aim to commit to a local church by the end of the first term and then aim to stay committed to it during the entire length of your course?

Some students are always away at weekends with sports, friends and family commitments. Perhaps aiming to return in time for the evening service could enable both commitments to be met.

Some students arrive late at church services (they slept in) and leave early (essay deadline). They sit with other students and know the name of the church pastor and no one else's. Their commitment to church is equivalent to that of the laundry run: a chore that needs to be done as quickly and as efficiently as possible. This is not good. Stay for coffee. Accept meal invitations. Invite people back. Make the church your spiritual family.

CHRISTIAN UNION

Saving Private Ryan is an epic war movie. We see the troops deployed at the Normandy beach landing, facing the unremitting hail of bullets and grenades. We see them support one another through the horror of trying to move through occupied France. They are men on a mission and so the fact that they are from very different social backgrounds, political persuasions and educational abilities doesn't matter. The mission unites them and they will live and die for one another to get the job done.

Many war veterans talk about the camaraderie of living on the front line; the acts of courage where individuals laid down their lives for people they had met only a few months previously. What they faced was horrific and yet the friendships forged were lifelong alliances.

Just like the squad in *Saving Private Ryan*, the CU has a mission that unites its members.

CUs have a unique and exciting part to play in university life, and all Christian students should belong to one. CUs are not seeking to be church, but to play a role as the church's missionary arm in the student subculture as they tailor strategies around students in a way that a local church cannot. Unfortunately CUs aren't perfect. Big CUs can make us feel anonymous. Small CUs can make us feel like we have just gate-crashed a stranger's hen night. Some are so different from our experience of church that we feel we have landed on a different planet. Sometimes the music is out of key, sometimes the speakers they dig up should have been left buried! Nevertheless it is vital for a Christian student to link in with their university CU.

The CU is a band of brothers and sisters called to fight the good fight of faith together. As we try to live for Christ and speak for Christ at university, our different church backgrounds and cultural heritages fade into the background. As our mission unites us, we support one another to live out Christ's calling on our lives. **Sometimes it will feel like a battle; sometimes like we are not going to make it; sometimes like the best place on earth to be.** It is when we lose sight of this mission that we become critical or complacent or cool in our faith.

The letter to the Hebrews was written to Christians whose faith was barely afloat. Originally aimed at a church context, the principles apply equally to Christian students and the CU. The writer offers us four healthy 'lettuces' (let us's) to help us stay faithful in a difficult environment:

Let us (1) hold unswervingly to the hope we profess, for he who promised is faithful. And let us (2) consider how we may spur one another on toward love and good deeds. Let us (3) not give up meeting together, as some are in the habit of doing, but let us (4) encourage one another – and all the more as you see the Day approaching. (Hebrews 10:23–25)

First, we are to hold unswervingly to the hope we have. Other passages of the Bible (for example, Romans 8:38–39) emphasize God holding on to us, but here we are told we have a responsibility to hold on ourselves.

Secondly, we are also responsible to help safeguard the faith of other Christians. If we choose not to join the CU, we might be abdicating our responsibility to help other students stay faithful to God.

Thirdly, we should do this by regularly meeting together. However big or small our CU, we can be encouraged by coming together to chat, pray, plan, read God's word and worship him.

Fourthly, we need to remember to make the effort to be encouraging: asking God for opportunities to encourage someone.

NINE REASONS TO JOIN THE CU:

1. CUs can provide the encouragement of knowing you are not alone on campus, but part of a larger group of believers standing for Christ.

2. CUs can provide inspiring main meetings where all the Christians come out of the woodwork to worship together.

3. CUs can adapt their form and style so that they connect relevantly and faithfully into the student subculture.

4. CUs can provide a forum for introducing students to the faith through outreach events, enquirer courses, mission meetings, etc.

5. CUs can provide opportunities to serve, whether through giving financially or practically or using your spiritual gifts.

6. CUs can provide real leadership opportunities. Led by students, for students, they offer a unique opportunity for leadership growth and development.

7. CUs can provide a taste of a time when denominations will no longer matter.

8. CUs can provide small groups with instant accountability, practice in leading Bible studies, and a chance to eat, pray and dream together.

9. CUs can provide an opportunity to connect with students nationally through the Universities and Colleges Christian Fellowship (www.uccf.org.uk) and internationally with the International Fellowship of Evangelical Students (www.ifesworld.org). Both these organizations provide staff and resources specifically to help and support students.

UNIVERSITY

There are many invisible people at university. The cleaner who checks our rooms, the cashier who sells us bread and milk at the campus grocery store, the librarian who passes over the reserved books, the porter who mans the college gate, the secretary of the department who signs for receipt of our assignments, the bus driver who drops us off at the lecture hall.

Most of our student life revolves around being with students, but being part of the university involves crossing paths on a daily basis with a much wider spectrum of the population. People with journeys and jobs, families and friends, hobbies and hassles. People whose daily responsibility it is to make life easier for us. What is our responsibility to them?

Leaving home and going off to university miles away may feel like a big step. Imagine being suddenly forcibly removed from home and sent to live in an oppressive country. The book of Jeremiah is written to the people of Judah, warning them that they will be exiled because of their disobedience to God. It is understandable that under those circumstances the Jews would have wanted to stick together and look out for their own needs. But the book of Jeremiah is full of encouragements that God was still in control, still with them, and still had a plan for them.

This is what the LORD Almighty, the God of Israel, says to all those I carried into exile from Jerusalem to Babylon: 'Build houses and settle down; plant gardens and eat what they produce. Marry and have sons and daughters; find wives for your sons and give your daughters in marriage, so that they too may have sons and daughters. Increase in number there; do not decrease. Also, seek the peace and prosperity of the city to which I have carried you into exile. Pray to the LORD for it, because if it prospers, you too will prosper.'
(Jeremiah 29:5–8)

Elsewhere God promises his people that he will eventually bring them home, but here he lets them know that this is not imminent. So he tells them to think long-term. These long-term plans involve finding homes and having children of their own, but they also involve the people around them. Although they were passing through, they were still called to be a blessing to Babylon.

There are many parallels to our life on earth as the people of God. We live in a world where governments, media and public life in general do not seek to please God. The church has little political clout and we can relate to the captives living in Babylon. God will eventually rescue us and bring us to the promised land of eternal life with him, but in the meantime, feeling like strangers passing through a strange land, we are called to be a blessing.

Throughout our lives, we should do all we can to bless our world, our nation, our neighbourhood, our families and friends. This is true while we are at university. Though we may well miss home and feel isolated and insignificant, we can take courage from Old Testament figures like Joseph and Daniel. These heroes of the faith apparently had no natural significance or power but, by being faithful to God they were able to make a huge impact on individuals and on the government and public life of the nations where they were slaves.

There are three key ways we can seek the welfare of the university and serve the invisible people.

GREET PEOPLE

Taking time to acknowledge people around us and take an interest in their lives stops them being invisible. It converts someone from being part of the furniture into a potential friend. It is a significant way to demonstrate God's love and bring a taste of his peace into our world. Many of us rush through life without investing time into those around us. Do we even say hello to the bar staff who serve our drinks, the guy who works in the kebab van, the IT helpdesk clerk who advises us how to set up our wireless connection, the doorman at the club? Do we know their names? Just saying good morning, asking how they are doing, and saying thank you, can be opportunities to bless.

GIVE RESPECT

Christians have a very high view of human life and the way we treat people demonstrates how we feel about the God we reflect. We can demonstrate the way God values all people as we interact with others. Do we pay our bills? Do our jokes demean people? Do we make sure we are at lectures on time? Do we leave our room reasonably tidy for the cleaner? Do our noise levels show respect for our neighbours? Do our headphones isolate us from others? Do we help clear up after CU meetings? Do we help others from different cultures? Do we respect those of different faiths?

GET INVOLVED

We see from Joseph and Daniel that God cares about the political realm. Even though God knew that the exiles were coming home, he still lined up a role for Daniel in the Babylonian government. Christians often get involved in politics on certain hot button issues: abortion, religious freedom, homosexuality, the status of the CU. These are important subjects and Christians ought to speak up and speak out. However we are also commanded to seek the welfare of the city. This means standing up for the needs of everyone on campus, not just rebuking those who do not live up to Christian standards. Opportunities to do this range from being a student course representative, a crèche volunteer, a blood donor, or president of the student union.

WEEK 3: EVANGELISM

UNIVERSITY CHALLENGE: WEEK 3

EXPRESSO CHALLENGE

Pledge to pray for five friends for the whole week.

Pray for opportunities to invite them to church or CU.
Pray for opportunities to share your faith story with them.
Pray for opportunities to demonstrate God's love to them.

EXTREME CHALLENGE

Update your Facebook/MySpace profile to include more details about your faith. Set a question such as 'What would you ask God?' or 'What would it take for you to seriously consider Christianity?' Follow up the responses with further discussion threads.

EXPRESSION CHALLENGE

Make a two-minute short movie about your journey to faith. Share it on YouTube and at www.freshspace.org.

WHY?

I once spent an hour digging through putrid food and stinking nappies. The neighbours probably thought I'd lost my marbles, but actually I had lost an envelope containing £50. The stench was awful but, motivated by the precious cash, I kept on hunting.

My passion to find lost pounds is nothing compared to God's passion to rescue lost people. Luke's Gospel records three stories back-to-back about 'lost things' (Luke 15). Three stories with the same theme ram the point home: we are supposed to pay very careful attention.

A shepherd notices that one of his sheep is missing and leaves the flock to hunt high and low until he finds it. It might seem ridiculous to leave ninety-nine to chase after one lost sheep. But the shepherd's joy at finding that sheep alive gives us a hint of how God feels over each one of us who repents.

A wife loses a precious coin. I love this story – it rings true, as I have heard of many girls who misplace their engagement rings! She turns the house upside down and when she eventually finds it, she doesn't clear up again, but throws a party for her friends. This party spirit is mirrored by God when someone who recognizes that they have messed up comes back to him.

Finally, a father loses his youngest son, not in some tragic accident, but because his son can't bear his company any more. Months later, this father sees his son limping home after blowing the family inheritance. He recognizes him, receives him, re-clothes him and reinstates him. No expense is spared for the welcome home party.

This last story has a twist. Some of us join in the party, rejoicing over the finding of lost things. Others of us are like the older brother who sits outside sulking and avoiding the celebration. The stories ask two questions. Do our hearts echo God's concern for lost people? Do we celebrate with him or sulk outside?

These stories are recorded in Luke's Gospel as a response to the criticism Jesus faced for hanging out with all the wrong kinds of people: social misfits, religious outcasts, spiritual losers, economic failures, morally bankrupt individuals (Luke 15:1–3). Why does Jesus spend time with the spiritually lost? It is because God is on a search-and-rescue mission for his lost people whom he loves and wants to bring home.

As Christians we have tasted God's incredible mercy. We have received the Father's welcome embrace. It is ridiculous to imagine that we could be like the older brother with no concern to share what we have with those who don't know Jesus.

Yet many of us struggle to share our faith. Maybe it is fear, maybe bad experiences, maybe a sense of unworthiness, or maybe we feel totally unequipped. We will explore ways to deal with this over the next few chapters. The aim of this chapter is for us to grasp that bringing lost people home is central to the heart of God. We may lack nerve, hope, skill or experience, but what we can't lack is motivation. Our chief aim in life as Christians is to please God. God the Father is most happy, we are told, when lost people come home. Let's join in God's party by doing whatever we can to be a part of the process of calling people back to God.

Levi the tax collector was called by Jesus and the next thing we hear is that he had arranged a dinner party for the other tax inspectors and bailiffs so they could be introduced to Jesus (Luke 5:27–32).

A thirsty and unpopular divorcee from Samaria decided to follow Jesus and rushed into town to tell anyone she could find to check Jesus out for themselves (John 4).

A quiet fisherman called Andrew met Jesus and immediately went to find his loud-mouthed brother and tell him the good news (John 1:35–42).

None of these New Testament characters needed much skill, training or arm-twisting to do effective evangelism. They were brand new Christians and acted on reflex to pass on what they had seen and heard. Their faith was contagious because they couldn't and didn't keep silent. They had discovered something worth sharing. As the Sri Lankan theologian D. T. Niles famously said, '**Evangelism is one beggar showing another beggar where to find bread.**'

The theologian J. I. Packer says that evangelism helps us to fulfil the two greatest commandments: loving God by making him happy by bringing lost people home to him; loving our neighbour by pointing them in the right direction to discover the good news of peace with God. Evangelism is at the centre of this book because it is at the centre of God's heart. It should be at the centre of our lives.

As I sat waist deep in rotten food, my clothes stained with unmentionably rank dustbin juice, I thought about how far God was willing to go to rescue lost people like you and me. He left the perfect cleanliness of heaven for a rotten world to find us. We should be prepared to go to any lengths to help bring his lost people home.

WHAT?

Our communal kitchen at university should have been condemned as a dangerous biohazard. Our cleaning lady on the other hand should have been offered the Queen's Award for bravery. Each day she fought the mess and returned the kitchen to order. Occasionally she decided to teach us the error of our slovenly ways by locking us out.

Looking back, it may have been for our own protection! In such an environment, I was confident that I could shine as a Christian. I walked around bubbling with positive energy and occasionally facing germ warfare for my flatmates by doing a whole pile of washing up by myself.

After ten weeks, I felt success was at hand when Sofie knocked on my door to say the words I had been waiting for. 'Krish, there's something different about you.' My heart skipped a beat. Finally, I thought, the smiles, scrubbing and sensitive pastoral care have paid off. Now I get to tell her about Jesus. What she actually said changed my life forever. 'I've noticed something that you do – it seems to give you a buzz – and I'm thinking of giving it a go. Where can I get hold of those vitamin C tablets you have?'

Two things happened as a result of that conversation. The first is that I stopped overdosing on vitamin C. My hero, Linus Pauling, the double Nobel Prize-winning chemist had recommended a 500 mg daily dose. But that was history. The second thing is that I stopped trying to do evangelism without words.

St Francis of Assisi is supposed to have coined the saying 'preach the gospel and use words if you have to'. This is becoming popular for Christians in our multicultural society where we feel we are not allowed to talk about what we believe. The problem with this approach is that it just doesn't work. People don't *guess* the gospel message from our actions. They put our behaviour down to a good upbringing, an unselfish gene, a personality trait – or multivitamins. What they need to know, they need to have explained in words.

Words and lifestyle go hand in hand. That was Paul's answer to his critics who challenged the way he did evangelism.

Because we loved you so much, we were delighted to share with you not only the gospel of God but our lives as well. (1 Thessalonians 2:8)

We can learn three key principles from Paul's evangelistic modus operandi:

Love is the motive, not guilt, fear, or intellectual one-upmanship. There was no church when Paul first went to Thessalonica, but Paul was delighted to show love to the strangers he met.

Words are necessary. Paul verbally explained the gospel of God. If anyone could have shown the gospel without words, it was Jesus. Jesus lived a perfect life but he was also a preacher. If it wasn't demeaning for Christ to speak to people about God, then it can't be so for us, and it certainly wasn't for Paul.

Lifestyle matters. Paul did not hold people at arm's length, but, again following Christ, allowed people close to him to share how the gospel worked out in practice. His lifestyle backed up his words.

Because we love God and the lost people he wants to find, we must speak the gospel, and we must live the gospel. There is no place quite like university for this. Living in close proximity to peers, and talking about everything under the sun, evangelism of life and lip should come naturally.

Here are three challenges:

TAKE A RISK

According to a recent survey, 3 million more people in the UK would go to church if a friend invited them.[2] I have met countless people who have turned up at Christian meetings just because someone had the courage to invite them along. Pray for an opportunity to invite a friend to something Christian this week.

TAKE THE OPPORTUNITY

We don't have to engineer bizarre ways of getting God into every conversation. Corny evangelistic chat-up lines which force a spiritual angle into an ordinary conversation can be unhelpful. Watch out for more natural opportunities like discussing the weekend. Alongside mentioning the hot date on Friday and the disappointing football match on Saturday, include the challenging sermon on Sunday. A brief honest sentence about church would nail our colours to the mast and give us the opportunity to see where the conversation goes next.

TAKE RESPONSIBILITY

If we don't pray and take opportunities to tell our friends and families about the gospel, who will? God in his wisdom and his grace has given us the privilege and responsibility of sharing the good news with people around us, by our lifestyles and by our words. Let's be people of integrity who decide to speak and live out the truth.

WHO?

'Evangelism isn't my thing. I'm just not Billy Graham. He could pack stadiums around the world for hours on end. Not me. I can clear a room in seconds just by opening my mouth about Jesus.'

The slick arena-filling preacher has become synonymous with evangelism, but the New Testament does not share this image of an evangelist. The Bible is clear that all of us have evangelistic responsibility. As we have seen, Bible evangelists include all sorts of personalities from very improbable backgrounds.

This means that for all Billy Graham's great work in the last century, we must learn not necessarily to associate a public figure, a loud voice and a polished presentation with evangelism. Peter was the stadium-filling evangelist on the day of Pentecost, but his brother Andrew was the one who quietly brought Peter to Jesus in the first place. Both Peter and Andrew, extrovert and introvert, public and private, were first-century evangelists. They had different, but significant, evangelistic ministries.

As we saw in the previous section, God created his church as a body with different parts and different gifts. This means God has made us the way we are to help bring lost people back to him. In order to be effective in evangelism, we do not need to conform to a certain set of stereotypical personality traits. Many of us excuse ourselves from doing evangelism because we don't have the personality and gift-mix normally associated with evangelists. We are not called to become different people in order to be used by God. We are called to make ourselves available to God just as he has made us.

God has placed us within certain unique friendship groups, families and relational networks. These people accept us for who we are and we are in a unique position to introduce them to Jesus.

God has placed us within certain Christian groups. Together as a body, we can help one another by the way our gifts fit together. Some of us find inviting people to events really easy, but we actually struggle when it comes to explaining the gospel or answering tough questions. Some of us are good at helping people to cross the line to faith and repentance, but are not good at the long-term follow up and discipleship. Some of us might long to help our friend cope with a family tragedy, but we can do this best by introducing her to another Christian who has had a similar experience. Working in teams helps us to make the most of our gifts and the gifts of others.

God has placed us strategically and we must learn to be content with the gifts and personalities he has given us, and to be humble as we work together with others. What a relief that we do not have to conform to a stereotype! But this is no excuse to be laid back with evangelism. Look what Paul says to Timothy:

For this reason I remind you to fan into flame the gift of God, which is in you through the laying on of my hands. For **God did not give us a spirit of timidity, but a spirit of power, of love and of self-discipline. So do not be ashamed to testify about our Lord**, *or ashamed of me his prisoner. But join with me in suffering for the gospel, by the power of God.* (2 Timothy 1:6–8)

If you have ever tried to get a fire going from some glowing embers you know how much effort it can take to get enough oxygen flowing so that the flame will be rekindled. Timothy is told he needs to work hard at keeping the gifts he has got operating at maximum effectiveness.

Timothy is a relatively young church leader whom Paul loved and treated like his own son. Paul knew that Timothy might be tempted to wish for different gifts than the ones he had been given. He knew that Timothy might be tempted to put his gifts to one side and let the dust gather, tempted to be ashamed and embarrassed about the gospel, tempted to run away from the difficulties rather than standing up for the good news.

Timothy is just like us! Paul reminds us that we must work hard and nurture our gifts by using them, despite all the temptations and difficulties. Paul also reminds us that the Holy Spirit inside every believer comes to give us power to face difficulties, love to motivate us to please God and the people around us, and self-discipline to persevere.

Most of us feel very nervous when we think about evangelism. But God has given us a unique relational network. He has given us a unique personality. He has given us unique gifts. He has placed us in a body of Christians with a uniquely complementary gift mix. He has given us a reminder to work hard to use our gifts, and he has given us the Holy Spirit to help us.

Whoever you are, you are called to be involved in evangelism. God has designed you uniquely. He has led your footsteps to a particular university, course, accommodation and friendship group. Whether you introduce hundreds to Jesus or just one person, you are destined to enjoy the pleasure of joining God's party, rejoicing over the lost coming home.

HOW?

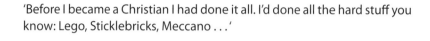

'Before I became a Christian I had done it all. I'd done all the hard stuff you know: Lego, Sticklebricks, Meccano . . .'

Simon was just not convinced that his conversion was exciting enough. He loved to hear about people who belonged to Hell's Angels and got into dangerous scrapes before they became Christians. He had heard several people give in-depth accounts of their drug trips before wowwing their audiences with the story of their miraculous transformation to Christianity. It seemed that everybody else had a life-story of their journey to Christ via crime, crack and a couple of ASBOs.

There is no such thing as a non-miraculous conversion. Paul tells us that before we became Christians we were spiritually dead (Ephesians 2:1) and blind (2 Corinthians 4:4). **All Christians have a life story that includes God's miraculous forgiveness**, and none of us should be ashamed of the momentous journey of how we came to accept God's grace.

When considering how we do evangelism, a good starting point is our own life story and journey to faith. In fact it is one of our most powerful evangelistic tools. People love to listen to human-interest stories. Our testimonies may be fascinating because they are dramatic or because they relate to the normal people around us. Either way, they give people a chance to see what the Christian faith really looks like. We all have a story to tell and can often gain a hearing where a preacher wouldn't.

There are plenty of opportunities to tell the story of how we became a Christian. It is highly likely that most of our friends will ask us at some point why we go to church, why we use different language from those around us, or why we care about 'that' guy or 'that' issue. It is worth giving some thought to how we might talk naturally, helpfully and clearly about our journey to faith.

Dan was the social secretary of the university rugby club. It was a role famed for promoting initiation rites, noise, vomit and unsociable behaviour. Perhaps it was a role that a Christian would choose to avoid. But Dan took up the job. While he was social secretary, freshers were protected from humiliation, and players got home safely from their drunken excursions. His lifestyle got him into plenty of trouble, but it also prompted people to ask why he was different. Dan was well practised at letting people know clearly why Jesus was at the centre of his life.

Evangelism got Paul in a lot of trouble. Eventually he was incarcerated and brought before the king to answer the charges against him. Paul was well practised at his testimony and told King Agrippa his gripping personal story.

Then Agrippa said to Paul, 'Do you think that in such a short time you can persuade me to be a Christian?' Paul replied, 'Short time or long – I pray to God that not only you but all who are listening to me today may become what I am, except for these chains.' (Acts 26:28–29)

Paul's story had a huge impact on King Agrippa and the other onlookers. As he used it to defend his faith, he knew that nobody could contradict him and that he would connect at a deeper level with those who heard him.

Your story belongs to you and you are the only expert on the subject. As people listen in, they can ask us questions, but they cannot disagree. Telling our stories also allows us to dispel myths that people may have about the Christian faith. It doesn't take much to incorporate an explanation that being a Christian is more than just being born into a Christian family or turning up at church, for example.

Whether we are expecting to be asked by royalty or by rugby mates, we should think ahead about what we will say. Here are some tips:

Although the story is about us, God needs to be the hero. We should be careful not to over-glorify our past life, or make it sound like we were so clever to find God or that God is so lucky to have us decide to follow him.

Although we need to be prepared, we should not go onto autopilot. Our stories should flow naturally into the conversation. This can happen by asking questions such as 'Have you ever felt like that?', or 'What's your experience of church?'

Although our story will involve sin, salvation and accepting Jesus as our Saviour, these words are just jargon to those outside of the faith. Talking to our mates, we need to phrase things carefully.

Although we will doubtless tell our stories repeatedly, we should be adaptable. It would be pretty weird to tell it the same way each time. Each time Paul tells his testimony, he covers the same ground but adapts it for his audience. Sometimes I tell my own testimony from the perspective of a Hindu background, or from the perspective of a science student or from the perspective of a struggling father.

However you tell your story, make sure you tell it often, faithfully and with a sense of bold humility. Humility because our relationship with God is not down to us but down to God's grace. Boldness because we do not need to be ashamed of the story of God's work in our life, even if it did begin when we were young enough to be into Lego and Sticklebricks.

WHEN?

Nikki didn't look her usual cheerful self. When I asked her how she was doing, she burst into tears. Half an hour later we were sitting having a coffee and she told me it was the anniversary of her sister's suicide. That was not the moment to launch into a sermon on someone who chose to die to give us life. That was a moment to listen and sympathize, to offer help and support. The opportunity to explain the gospel message came a few weeks later.

We were in the common room. It was minutes to midnight and we had all just been to see a movie about life after death. It had everyone talking. Finally someone asked me 'What did you make of it, Krish?' I dropped a gospel idea into the discussion. We ended up talking about the fact that Christians believe in life after death because of Jesus' resurrection.

Be wise in the way you act toward outsiders; make the most of every opportunity. **Let your conversation be always full of grace, seasoned with salt, so that you may know how to answer everyone.** (Colossians 4:5–6)

Making the most of every opportunity means that we never go off duty as Christians. Just as Christ lived the gospel 24/7 so we are called to do the same. It means knowing the right time to speak and when to say silent. It means knowing when to drop hints, ask questions or give straight answers.

Evangelism can take place for different reasons.

WHEN WE ARE ASKED WHY WE ARE DIFFERENT

We saw in the last chapter that telling our story is a great way to explain the difference that knowing God makes to our lives. During other conversations we can drop in comments or questions. People may pick up on it at the time or later. My dentist asked me why I had a T-shirt with Dr Martin Luther King on it. I just said I was inspired by a man who put his Christian faith into action. I sowed the idea and I left it hanging. I couldn't have said anything else anyway – I had a numb mouth and a drill down my throat! But perhaps on my next visit we can take it further.

WHEN WE ARE ASKED OUR OPINIONS

The other day someone asked me what was my favourite film of all time. I told them it was *The Shawshank Redemption* because it has a lot of parallels with the Christian faith. Again I paused to see if they wanted to pursue that conversation or not. As we watch the news, listen to music, or read novels, people will naturally ask us our opinions. It's a great opportunity to talk about big ideas and sow a seed about the gospel.

WHEN WE ARE ASKED TRICKY QUESTIONS

Paul assumes people are going to ask us questions. We need to know how to 'give an answer to everyone' as Peter tells us (1 Peter 3:15). Unfortunately the questions are often more tricky than 'What is your favourite film?'. None of us is omniscient, so it is true that there will be many questions to which we do not have an answer. When someone asks us a tough question, we must try not to panic but to do the following things:

LISTEN

Listen to the Holy Spirit and ask him for discernment and wisdom (Luke 12:11–12).

Listen to the questioner. People ask questions for many reasons. Sometimes they want to catch us out. Sometimes they want to avoid facing the truth. Sometimes they want to test the water before asking the real question. Sometimes they desperately need help with a very real struggle. A hot potato topic such as a Christian response to homosexuality or abortion could come under any of these categories. Delving around the question before attempting an answer can not only buy valuable thinking time but also establish a rapport with the questioner and establish what is really going on in his or her mind.

GIVE IT YOUR BEST SHOT

Do your best with God's strength to give an answer that will both honour God and help the listener. Try to draw people back to the gospel, and avoid taking sides on divisive issues that will distract people from the core truths of the Christian faith.

BE HONEST

Admitting we don't know an answer shows humility, and a willingness to do some research shows interest. We gain more credibility for the gospel by going down this route than by blagging it. Following up the discussion later is an opportunity to show love in action.

WHERE?

Jim Elliot was a student ablaze for God. He felt God's call to take the gospel to the ends of the earth. He took up wrestling at university to make himself physically tougher to face the wilds of the mission field. Eventually he went to South America and was martyred aged 28 as he attempted to bring the gospel to a tribe which had had no previous contact with Christianity. In the end, through the work of Jim Elliot's wife Elizabeth, seven of the nine killers were converted. Elliot had prophetically written in his journal, **'He is no fool who gives up what he cannot keep to gain what he cannot lose.'**

I love reading missionary biographies like Elliot's. Hudson Taylor, William Carey, Amy Carmichael and others have moved, inspired and challenged me by their heroic stories. If you ever see my copies, you will find them filled with passages marked with yellow highlighter pen. Each missionary had incredible bravery, language skills, patience, cultural insight or preaching abilities. Each one makes me feel very small, insignificant and under-qualified.

While recognizing the great debt I owe to these incredible men and women, the picture of mission they portray is too small. The New Testament's approach to global mission is even bigger, and we are all invited and resourced to get involved.

Jesus was a missionary because God sent him on a mission to live, die and rise again for the sins of the world.

The global church is missionary because Jesus sends it out to be part of God's mission to bring back lost people. Mission is the very reason the church exists and it incorporates all we do to beam the message out. This includes feeding the hungry, speaking out for the voiceless, proclaiming the gospel, caring for the environment and seeking the welfare of the places where we live, just as Jesus did.

Each Christian is a missionary because we are members of God's church. Whatever we choose to do with our lives, we must consider how we can use our gifts and skills for God's purposes in the world (Matthew 6:33). Becoming an accountant is more than playing with figures. It is more than supporting our dependants. It is more than supporting the local church. It spills over into supporting global mission when we choose to honour God in our day-to-day work: helping people be good stewards of their finances or climb out of debt is mission. Treating clients well, praying for them, and speaking out for the gospel is all mission.

Mission is when we do what God wants us to do in his universe. Accountants, nurses, teachers, TV presenters, mothers, politicians and taxi drivers can all be effective missionaries in the world through their vocations in the communities to which God sends them.

God sends some of us to be missionaries in our own countries and others to be missionaries abroad, scattering us out to the very ends of the world, just as Jesus prophesied after his death and resurrection:

But you will receive power when the Holy Spirit comes on you; and you will be my witnesses in Jerusalem, and in all Judea and Samaria, and to the ends of the earth. (Acts 1:8)

The gospel was going global, and the first disciples who had thought that neighbouring Samaria was a long way from home could not comprehend it when they were told that they were going to take the message to the ends of the earth. They had no idea of the planet's geography. They had no idea of probable martyrdom.

Those first disciples were ambassadors for God's peace but most were killed for proclaiming God's message of reconciliation. This mission was impossible without the filling of the Holy Spirit, and that same Holy Spirit is at work today, filling us with the power we need to continue God's mission to the world.

As students we have some amazing opportunities. The UK has the second largest number of international students after America. Approximately one in seven students is an international, including around 200,000 from outside of the European Union.[3] Many come from places where evangelism is illegal. The ends of the earth have come to us and we have a responsibility to show authentic love and genuine friendship. Look out for the CU's ministry to international students, and for the work of Friends International which specializes in international student outreach.

Whilst at university, we have more holiday time than at any other point in our life. Setting apart some of it to invest in the global church will make a big impact on those we serve and on our awareness of the church worldwide. If holidays are still not long enough, why not consider a gap year before or after university?

There are even programmes which will pay for us to study at universities abroad. Look out for the Erasmus scheme, twinning schemes, foreign electives and exchange years, which provide an amazing opportunity to experience another culture, learn another language, discover how to do ministry in another context, and serve the global church.

WHAT NEXT?

I still remember my school sports day in July 1987. I was to run the glory leg of the four-by-100 m relay race. The starter's gun fired and we were off. The first leg runner got us off to a great start. The changeover was perfectly smooth. The second leg runner was powering around the corner. Another faultless changeover gave our third runner a chance to shine. I could see him steaming down the back straight, a picture of concentration and dedication, eyes focused, muscles straining, baton in hand. I set off, arm outstretched, ready to receive the baton. By the time I realized that I was in the wrong lane, it was all over and we were disqualified.

Everybody's effort and energy had been wasted, because of me. The chain broke and I learned a painful lesson. When Jesus passed on the baton of the gospel, it managed to get all the way to me. My spiritual heritage is an unbroken chain of people who passed on that baton. I am determined that the chain reaction of gospel communication will not end with me in the same way as the relay race.

To make doubly sure we are in the right lane, we need to check the starter's block. Right at the beginning, Jesus handed over the baton with his great commission.

Then the eleven disciples went to Galilee, to the mountain where Jesus had told them to go. When they saw him, they worshipped him; but some doubted. Then Jesus came to them and said, 'All authority in heaven and on earth has been given to me. **Therefore go and make disciples of all nations, baptizing them in the name of the Father and of the Son and of the Holy Spirit, and teaching them to obey everything I have commanded you.** *And surely I am with you always, to the very end of the age.'* (Matthew 28:16–20)

Here we see Jesus sending his disciples out on their global mission. It is a classic text for evangelism. However this passage is about more than evangelism – it is about disciple-making. Let's take a closer look.

SOME WITH DOUBTS

Even after witnessing the death and resurrection of Jesus, some disciples doubt. Even in the presence of the risen Lord, some doubt. We can be encouraged that doubts do not disqualify us from ministry.

SENT WITH AUTHORITY

Jesus states that he is fully in charge. God does not need us; he is perfectly able to do his work himself. But God chooses to use defective disciples for his perfect purposes, so that we grow close to him, become like him and demonstrate his grace. When we dare to share the message of Jesus we are backed by the authority of heaven.

SENT TO ALL NATIONS

The gospel was always for the entire world. It is because the original disciples were faithful that the message came to us. We need to be part of this historic global chain reaction so that the message gets to every human being.

SENT TO MAKE DISCIPLES

Followers of Jesus are to be baptized into the name of the Triune God: Father, Son and Holy Spirit. We are to be taught the gospel, but this is more than just a transmission of data about Jesus. We must learn to obey everything that Christ commanded. By implication we must also learn to obey this last command of Jesus: to go and make disciples of all nations and to teach them to obey. The chain of disciple-making needs to continue, generation after generation.

SENT WITH THE PRESENCE OF JESUS

Jesus promises his presence with us, to the very end of the age. We know that he is with us in the person of the Holy Spirit. It is God's Spirit that gives us the comfort and confidence we need to go to the ends of the earth and make disciples for Christ.

When we consider our own Christian growth, there are probably several influential people who have helped. Perhaps a youth leader, friend, teacher, pastor or parent who has given us time, energy and love. We need to make sure that we are still growing as Christians and learning from more mature disciples. Look out for and appreciate people who spend time with you, checking how you are doing, answering your difficult questions. Make sure that the chain link holding you in place is strong.

But the command given by Jesus is not to be a disciple but to make disciples, and as followers of Christ we are called to mentor others in their faith. We need to form strong links with younger Christians, helping them to grow. By meeting to study the Bible, pray and do ministry together regularly, we are learning to obey Jesus' great commission.

Don't drop the baton.

WEEK 4: STUDIES

EXPRESSO CHALLENGE

List five hopes you have for your studies:

1.

2.

3.

4.

5.

Share them on www.freshspace.org and email the link to a friend back home and ask them to pray with you for them.

EXTREME CHALLENGE

Order one Christian book that relates to your field of study and pledge to read it before Christmas (you'll find a list of recommended books at www.freshspace.org).

OR

Join a professional group relating to your field of study (see www.freshspace.org).

OR

Find some other Christians on your course and arrange to pray together each fortnight for issues relating to your studies and for the people in your department.

EXPRESSION CHALLENGE

Write a 500-word posting on how you could expect to discover God in your studies, and how you could grow as a Christian as you become more expert in your academic field. Share it online on www.freshspace.org.

> The more I study, the more I know.
> The more I know, the more I forget.
> The more I forget, the less I know.
> So why study?

That is the existential excuse for not studying.

Here is a Christian argument:

More than 40,000 children starve to death each day. I should not waste precious time and resources conjugating verbs or learning about noble gases. More people than I can count are slipping into the darkness without knowing Christ. Surely every waking hour we have should be spent helping people learning about Christ, not logging on at the library or writing essays. The more I study, the less I do God's work. So why study?

REASON 1: STUDY IS A LEGITIMATE USE OF TIME

Jesus attended weddings and parties. He slept soundly and did not live life in a mad rush to reach the world. In fact, when things got frantic, he took his disciples away so they could relax and learn in a more exclusive environment. We are obviously not meant to live life in an anxious panic for God. As Jesus died on the cross he said, 'It is finished.' Jesus did not accomplish everything on earth that needed doing – there were still many lost people, many sick people. But his part of the mission was complete. We are not responsible for the whole of God's mission. But we do need to do our part.

REASON 2: STUDY IS MINISTRY

God has given us an appetite to work things out, put ideas together, research, summarize, and to shine. We may not think of ourselves as academics or intellectuals, but we definitely have some sort of academic gifts. At the start of World War II, C. S. Lewis preached a sermon helping students to realize that those at university were playing just as an important role as those on the battlefield:

'An appetite for these things exists in the human mind, and God makes no appetite in vain. **We can therefore pursue knowledge as such, and beauty, as such, in the sure confidence that by so doing we are either advancing to the vision of God ourselves or indirectly helping others to do so . . .** ' [4]

REASON 3: STUDY SHARPENS OUR GOD-GIVEN SKILLS

Imagine the opening scenes of a James Bond movie. Bond always visits Q to collect his equipment: the car with the ejector seat, the watch with the laser beam, the pen with a bomb inside. We pay particular attention at this point because we know that he is going to need every last one of those secret agent toys in order to fulfil his mission. The same is true of the gifts God has given us by his grace. Pay attention. We will undoubtedly be learning something at university that will be used to complete the mission God has for our life.

REASON 4: STUDY HELPS US LOVE GOD

Lewis went on to say: 'The intellectual life is not the only road to God, nor the safest, but we find it to be a road, and it may be the appointed road for us . . .'[4]

Study is not only useful for our own development and for God's own mission, but it is also useful for our relationship with God. Studying God's universe will help us appreciate him more. A musician can honour God through composing beautiful music even if that music is only heard in the practice studio. Solving complex calculus, appreciating a classic piece of literature, struggling with the failings of world politics, can similarly make us marvel at God and thus these become acts of worship.

We might think that in the grand scheme of things, writing up an assignment or attending a lecture is as trivial as eating beans on toast or having a beer with a mate. Surely the Bible doesn't have anything to say about these mundane everyday activities? But Paul writes:

So whether you eat or drink or whatever you do, do it all for the glory of God. (1 Corinthians 10:31)

Paul writes this to a church where there is some controversy about whether meat offered to idols is a big deal or not. Basically Paul's answer enables us to see that our food, drink, calculus, music, assignments, attendance, chilling with mates or sweating it out at the gym can all be worship to God if we offer it to him for his glory. God can turn the mundane into the sublime.

SO WHY BOTHER?

The more I study, the more I learn about God. The more I learn about God, the more I worship him. The more I worship him, the more I want to please him in everything I do. The more I try to please him, the more I realize I need to learn more . . .

So study!

He had told his wife that he was an undercover agent working for a secret government security agency. Because of his work he often had to spend time away from his family and would be completely out of contact. When the truth eventually came out the newspaper reported that this man was indeed living a double life, but of a different sort. Across town he had another wife and another family, who also believed he was a secret agent.

The man was so practised in his lies, they sounded utterly believable. He was living life at an unreal pace, keeping two wives and his real job completely separate. Living an honest life would have been so much simpler. Eventually his juggling act had to end in disaster. His wives were so totally unaware of his secret that they were devastated when they discovered the truth.

Many of us try to live double lives. We have a spiritual self that goes to church and CU, prays and reads the Bible. We also have an academic self that goes to lectures, writes essays and reads journals. Each self has its own set of friends, habits and even language. We think that life would be less complicated if they never overlapped, but actually managing multiple identities is a juggling act that normally ends in disaster. God calls us to be men and women of integrity, and to make sure that we find a way to live effectively and worship as academic believers and believers in the academy.

Is God interested in the evangelism that we do after lectures but not what we are doing in the lectures themselves? Before we step into a tutorial or a lab, do we leave God at the door and pick him up again at the end of the day? Does God vanish when we open a textbook and reappear when we open our Bible?

The God who created the mind deserves to be the centre of our lives all the time – the spiritual time and the secular time. This means that secular time is actually spiritual time and secular study spiritual learning. All of our time is an opportunity to worship.

We meet God in our course reading, and we also meet our studies in God's word.

Who has measured the waters in the hollow of his hand,
*   or with the breadth of his hand marked off the heavens?*
Who has held the dust of the earth in a basket,
*   or weighed the mountains on the scales*
*   and the hills in a balance?*

Who can fathom the Spirit of the LORD,
  or instructed the LORD as his counsellor?
Whom did the LORD consult to enlighten him,
  and who taught him the right way?
Who was it that taught him knowledge,
  or showed him the path of understanding?
(Isaiah 40:12–14)

The Bible teaches that God's understanding far outweighs anything we will ever learn. None of us can boast the technical ability of God. No scientist can know more about the universe. No psychologist will ever come near what God knows about the human mind. No biologist will ever be able to tell us how many hairs are on our head. No historian will ever be able to see human history from beginning to end. No geographer will ever hold the contours of the world in his hand. No designer will ever create galaxies or entire species of creatures. No author can compare with the author of life itself.

I am not saying the Bible contains solutions to computer coding assignments or theories of Australian marine development. But becoming voracious readers of the Bible will give us a perspective on the universe so that we can approach our studies with wisdom. Christians know where learning began. We know where it will end. We also know its limitations. Soaking our minds in Scripture and obeying Scripture will give us the ability to see things about the universe that even our non-Christian lecturers will miss.

Your commands are always with me
   and make me wiser than my enemies.
I have more insight than all my teachers,
   for I meditate on your statutes.
I have more understanding than the elders,
   for I obey your precepts.
(Psalm 119:98–100)

Some students focus on their studies at the expense of all other areas of their life. Other students put studies at the bottom of their priorities – they attend university for the social life. As Christians we must not fall into either trap. We must be students of God's wisdom and enjoy discovering God and his universe on our course-reading, and in our Bible-reading.

Jesus is Lord not just of our hearts but over all creation. To be a Christian student means to allow Christ to rule over our minds as well as our hearts and lives. Abraham Kuyper was a theologian. He was also prime minister of Holland. When he founded the Free University of Amsterdam, he declared:

'No single piece of our mental world is to be hermetically sealed off from the rest, and there is not a square inch in the whole domain of our human existence over which Christ, who is Sovereign over all, does not cry: "Mine!"'[5]

Slaving away over that essay at 3 am in the morning. Six empty coke cans on the desk beside you along with several overdue library books. You can see which of your friends are still online and some of them are trying to distract you. You know you need to meet that 9 am deadline but the word count is still way off the mark, and if the assignment is not finished, you are dead meat.

Work feels like a nuisance at university. It interferes with our social life and is much more complicated than A levels. We feel like slaves, working hard without a penny to show for it.

We may feel like slaves, but we are not. We have the freedom to be able to choose if, what and where we study, and the ability to find a way to pay for it. Real slaves dare not even dream of such privileges.

Slavery is an evil that has existed from antiquity and is still with us. In fact there are more people living as slaves today than at any time in human history.[6] Traded as commodities rather than valued as people, slavery is a dehumanizing form of oppression. In his letter to the Colossian church, Paul does not consider it beneath him to write something especially to and for slaves. And what he writes is gold dust because what slaves don't get is dignity. But it is dignity that Paul is offering them for their diligence.

Slaves, obey your earthly masters in everything; and do it, not only when their eye is on you and to curry their favour, but with sincerity of heart and reverence for the Lord. Whatever you do, work at it with all your heart, as working for the Lord, not for human masters, since you know that you will receive an inheritance from the Lord as a reward. It is the Lord Christ you are serving. (Colossians 3:22–24)

As freshers, we may feel we are bottom of the food-chain, out of our depth with our workload and easy pickings for the university authorities, tutors and lecturers. When we feel pushed beyond our physical and mental capabilities, we can draw encouragement from this passage.

First of all, Paul addresses the slaves as members of the family. Whatever society said about slaves, Paul knew they were his brothers and sisters in Christ and his co-heirs in eternity. When we feel most alone at university, outside our natural family unit, we can take great comfort in knowing that we are amongst equals in God's family.

Secondly, Paul tells slaves that heaven will not be their first opportunity to honour God. In their slave labour, they can worship God.

Thirdly, Paul offers slaves a new perspective on their identity. Although they may be branded with their earthly master's name on their skin, their true heart allegiance is to God. This makes the most tedious and tiresome task significant. As we type the name of the tutor on the cover sheet of the assignment, we know that our paper is for God first and foremost.

Fourthly, Paul reminds slaves that someone is watching. Although they may seem invisible to society, working behind the scenes without acknowledgement or remuneration, God is taking note and preparing a reward. As we type away late at night, or as we get back a paper with a low grade, it is easy to feel that nobody is watching the effort we are putting in. Knowing we are working for the Lord drives us forward.

Finally, Paul encourages slaves that their heart attitude to those they are serving matters as much as the quality of their work. If this applies to slaves in forced labour, how much more does it apply to us as freely-choosing students! **Gaining a First at the end of the course is not our ultimate goal. Our aim is to honour God by doing our best.**

I once saw a book called *How to Survive University as a Christian*. The title unfortunately suggests that university is a dangerous place for faith, an idea that is echoed by many Christians. They feel their faith could easily be destroyed by academic study or carnal temptations, and so our best hope is just to survive.

Paul could easily have taken this line with the slaves. He could have told them just to hang in there as long as possible, and perhaps their faith might just survive the terrible conditions. Paul's attitude is more about thriving than surviving. Slaves could fully experience the amazing fact of God's acceptance. They could fully appreciate the significance of obeying God. They could fully participate in worship. They could fully enjoy God's presence. And they could fully anticipate God's reward.

Our faith can thrive at university. Away from home we can find incredible strength from knowing that we belong to God's family. We can forge a new identity, seeking to please God, as well as our tutors. We can learn what it means to really worship God with our whole lives, with our work and with our future.

What we can learn from the slaves in this passage is the discipline of diligence – not a popular term, but a godly one. When family, friends and tutors are not watching, we can choose to do our best for God and offer this to him as worship.

> The Matrix is everywhere. It's all around us, even in this very room. You can see it when you look out your window or when you turn on your television. You can feel it when you go to work, when you go to church, when you pay your taxes. The Matrix is the world that has been pulled over your eyes, to blind you from the truth.[7]

The Matrix is one of my favourite movies. I have seen it more times than I dare to mention and I covet Morpheus's shades. The concept of the 'matrix' as a projected virtual reality that stops us from seeing the world as it is has a philosophical parallel. We all have a worldview that filters the way we look at the world around us. It is there when we go to lectures, cook our dinner or go out for a drink. A worldview is the set of assumptions and values which has been pulled over our eyes. It is affected by our education, family life, church, the media. And it affects our outlook on the whole of life. Most of us are not aware of our worldview. It is like wearing Morpheus' sunglasses – we look through them rather than at them.

When we move from home to university, we have a brief period when we become more aware of our worldview. When we arrive in a lecture, canteen or common room we suddenly come across people with very different sets of assumptions. There is often a clash of worldviews.

Take the following examples:

While the students are watching the news in the common room, a discussion begins about political intervention. It becomes clear that Barratt believes that countries should be left to sort out their own problems. This is due to his family's experiences. His strong personality wins over the popular opinion. Later that evening, a girl is heard crying in her room, but nobody goes in to help because Barratt says to leave her alone. As a Christian, Rina feels the conflict at the political level (with the initial discussion), the personal level (with Barratt), the social level (with her friends) and the pastoral level (with the girl).

Jem is intrigued when his literature lecture focuses on biblical imagery. However it is clear that his tutor does not believe in God and has a negative angle on Christianity. He concludes that the deaths of Jesus in the Bible and the hero in the novel are both meaningless acts. Jem is concerned that he did not speak out in the tutorial. He is also afraid that his course peers have no respect for Christians after the tutorial. Finally, he realizes that he is expected to write an essay on the subject which his atheist tutor will assess and mark.

Different worldviews have fundamentally different assumptions. Some people believe we are intrinsically valuable, others that we are worthless. Some believe that we are basically good, others that we are fundamentally bad; some that the world is getting better, others that the world is getting worse. These assumptions have implications for the way we look at what is happening in the world, the way we treat people and the way we make decisions.

Whatever we study or discuss, we will eventually come across conflicts that stem from these initial assumptions. The typical conflicts range from the origins of the universe for the scientist, sanctity of life for the medic, or the problem of good and evil for the drama student.

There are two distinct ways that we can take advantage of worldview conflicts. By exploring worldview differences instead of running away from them, we can first of all help others to see the assumptions behind their opinions. Secondly we can add breadth and depth to our own understanding and explanation of our faith. Both can work together to make our studies an opportunity to honour God.

For though we live in the world, we do not wage war as the world does. The weapons we fight with are not the weapons of the world. On the contrary, they have divine power to demolish strongholds. We demolish arguments and every pretension that sets itself up against the knowledge

of God, and we take captive every thought to make it obedient to Christ.
(2 Corinthians 10:3–5)

Paul acknowledges that there is often a conflict between Christian and non-Christian ways of thinking. He also reminds us that this is not a physical warfare – there should be no guns or grenades launched in the name of Christ. It is an unequivocal doctrine of the Christian faith that we are called to love our neighbours, and love and do good to our enemies. But out of love for others we may need to engage in debate. **Through persuasion, proclamation, discussion and argument Christians should challenge systems of thought that are against God in order to liberate people from lies and bring the truth of Christ to all.** Morpheus in *The Matrix* has a similar mission. The truth shall set us and others free.

Jem and Rina are both in an unenviable position. They both need to be courageous: Jem in his seminar and Rina in her common room. But they need to do this in great humility, showing love and gentleness, and a willingness to learn. By asking a few key questions, they could expose some false assumptions. By writing a well-thought-out essay, or by deliberately helping the girl in tears, they have the opportunity to demonstrate the truth of the Christian worldview.

Time is money: we invest time, save time, lose time, spend time, redeem time, waste time. We talk as if we could control time in the same way we can control our finances. But whatever we do, we all have the same twenty-four hours in a day.

Nevertheless the financial language about time is useful. We are accountable to God for the time he has entrusted us with, and we need to manage it wisely. Jesus told a story about a man who entrusted three servants with eight bags of money (Matthew 25:14–30). Two servants doubled their investments of five and two bags. The other, given one bag, refused to invest and simply buried it. When the master returned, he rewarded the first two servants, but the third owned up, saying, 'I knew that you are a hard man, harvesting where you have not sown and gathering where you have not scattered seed' (verse 24). The third servant was disciplined and held accountable for his laziness.

God entrusts us with spiritual gifts, natural talents, academic ability, technical skills, relational resources and the gift of time. None of these belong to us. God has been generous and empowering by trusting us to look after his resources. But refusing to use our gifts is effectively accusing him of being a hard and exploitative master.

So how can we use our time well, as good stewards of each twenty-four-hour day he gives us?

TIME IS PRECIOUS

We would love to make every second count for God. But we are in danger of being too busy. Jesus did not live life in a frantic rush. He gently completed all he had to do in thirty-three years and then breathed 'it is finished' at the end of his life. Society may believe that life is about squeezing in as much as possible. Christians may think that we need to do the same and go to church and save the world, but Jesus' example teaches us to trust God's timings and do what we can in the time we have got.

TIME TO REST

One way we can demonstrate faith in God is through taking adequate rest. God has given us a pattern so that we can understand that our time is in his hands, but also so that we might get the most out of our time on earth. Leaving home for the first time and going to university gives us a fresh start to get this right.

Six days you shall labour and do all your work, but the seventh day is a Sabbath to the Lord your God. On it you shall not do any work, neither you, nor your son or daughter, nor your male or female servant, nor your ox, your donkey or any of your animals, nor any foreigner within your gates, so that your male and female servants may rest, as you do. (Deuteronomy 5:13–14)

Author, pastor and video producer Rob Bell comments that as slaves, the people of Israel were defined by what they produced. If they did not produce enough bricks, they would be beaten by their slave masters.[8] But here God demonstrates to his people that their worth was not dependent on what they made.

The Sabbath puts work back into perspective. Choosing one day when we do no course work, revision or essays could be a powerful sign. It signals to our friends that our primary identity is not as a student but as a child of God. It signals that although we take our studies seriously, we do so out of reverence for God.

This pattern is healthy, allowing us to re-energize and enjoy the good things God has made. Admittedly it is a difficult discipline to keep up, especially when essay deadlines loom and during exam time. But perhaps one day off is even more important during those pressure times.

TIME TO WORK

Rest teaches us not to dishonour God with workaholism, where work has become more important than God. On the other hand, laziness, or being idle, are the equal and opposite dangers to making work our idol.

Treating our studies as a full-time job is helpful. A Monday to Friday 9-to-5 week of forty hours is a good aim. Fitting in library slots between lectures has the potential benefit of leaving evenings and weekends work free and leaving us with a clear conscience. Another pattern is to divide the day into three time slots: eight hours to sleep, eight hours to study, eight hours for everything else.

We may feel busy, but the flexibility of time at university is unparalleled in the rest of life. **Getting a good balance between work and rest, Christian friends and other friends, sleep and social life is part of the university challenge.** Why not audit your time this week? Then reflect on how you can spend it more wisely.

CRAMMING AND WRITING

There were tears in my first lecture. We were thrown in at the deep end, and not many of us could swim. A lecturer who spoke as if we weren't even there spent the entire fifty minutes talking gibberish to the whiteboard. The first equation he wrote down gave me arm ache from copying it. So that's what physical chemistry was going to be – physical pain.

Studying is not normally physically painful, but it can cause a lot of emotional pain and stress. Writing essays and preparing for exams are two of the most stressful things we do as students.

The Bible does not provide a template for writing the perfect essay, nor does it give ten handy tips for cramming for exams. However it does provide a framework for us to approach these two pressure points.

GOD IS THE ULTIMATE EXAMINER

In the end, it is God's evaluation of our lives that matters most, more important than the grades we get or the degrees we earn. The Bible teaches us the value of a clear conscience. Doing our best before God, both in our studies and in the way we live for him, is what we will be judged on at the end of time.

GOD GIVES US PERSPECTIVE

There is something about being away from home and surrounded by a whole campus full of people worrying about essays and exams that can make us lose perspective and become obsessive. Taking a Sabbath rest can be a helpful countermeasure to stress, as can getting involved with a local church where people are facing a wider variety of life issues. In my final year, I was part of a church house group. One of the members was diagnosed with cancer, and another family was struggling with a miscarriage. That really put my stress into perspective. God can be trusted. Future security in life is not dependent on exam success.

GOD CALLS US TO BE GENEROUS

Exam stress can bring out the worst in people. We can be short-tempered. We can be miserly with our time because we feel we need to have our heads in our books. We can become competitive and jealous. We can become oblivious to the people around us.

Christian generosity can be highly prophetic during these times. If we take time to share our studies with others, we can demonstrate Christ's selflessness. If we take time out of studies to offer somebody practical help, this demonstrates something of Christ's compassion. We may need to start our essays and revision early to free up time to do this. Whatever the sacrifice, the people around us are worth the cost.

GOD CALLS US TO WORK HARD

Excellence is always worth pursuing. God has created us for good works and, as we labour for him in our relationships and in our studies, we know we are pleasing him.

GOD CALLS US TO CHALLENGE THE NORMS

We can use some essays to challenge the secular assumptions of our discipline. It could be an exploration of the relationship between faith and science. It could be the use of biblical images in literature. It could be research into Christian approaches to psychology. Perhaps we could aim to write one essay along these lines during our university career for the following reasons:

1. It would help us think in a systematically Christian way about our subject.
2. It would be a form of outreach to the college.
3. It would sharpen our apologetic skills.
4. It would nail our colours to the mast in our area of study.
5. It would test out a calling of whether we might be called to go into further academic study.

Some readers might be concerned that we may receive bad marks for such an essay. However lecturers often like to read a well-argued essay from an unusual position. It is like a breath of fresh air during marking hundreds of similar essays.

Author T. R. Glover once asked: 'How did the Church, confronted by the power of Greek philosophy, Roman might, and unchecked sensuality change the direction of world history? They out-lived the pagans, out-died them, and out-thought them.'[9]

In our mission to the university we too must be prepared to out-live, out-die and out-think our non-Christian institutions.

Jo went to university because she was passionate about showing God's love by bringing clean water to African villages. She trained to be an engineer and used each summer vacation to gain serious field experience. Tony went to study law, because he wanted to share God's heart for justice in the world and especially to defend the cause of the poor, weak and unjustly treated. Esta knew that God had given her a gift to relate to children and so she went to teacher training college.

Of course we are not all so clear about what God is calling us to. We choose what we study because we like the subject, because our parents have guided us, or because the prospectus made it sound exciting. Perhaps we are trying to discover what God wants to do with our lives. Or perhaps we drifted into university and expect to drift into a career afterwards.

But it is helpful to pause and reflect before drifting – or careering – into a lifetime of work. How we see work is critical. Is it something we do to pay the bills and prevent us from getting bored with life? This is the approach that our culture takes, seeing work simply as a job. Or do we, like Jo, Tony and Esta, see work as a vocation, something we do with the express intention of seeking to serve and honour God?

Knowing what work God is calling us into helps us focus at university. It helps us to begin to think through the ethical and practical issues we might face. It helps us begin to network with other Christians in our discipline. It helps us know whether we need to pursue postgraduate training or vacation apprenticeships. Professional Christian groups in the workplace are often very happy to link in with students aiming to join them after university (see the Fresh website: www.freshspace.org).

For some of us, God has not yet revealed his long-term plans for us. Joseph, learning to keep house for Potiphar, had no idea he would one day be Egypt's prime minister. Luke, studying medicine, had no idea he would also become one of the world's best-known authors. Paul, studying under Gamaliel, had no idea God would call him to preach the gospel to the Gentiles.

By keeping our ears open to God's call, we must follow Joseph, Luke and Paul's examples to try to honour God in all we do, and be prepared to change course when we hear it.

Some Christians live as if there is some kind of moral pecking order of acceptable vocations. A preacher comes top of the pile, followed by cross-cultural missionaries, followed by those in caring professions, followed by everybody else. The Bible knows nothing of this spiritual hierarchy and instead talks of the body where each gift is of equal value and no one can look down on anyone else. We need to continue to rediscover the role of well-informed Christians in the workplace and in public life.

Esther was an attractive Jewish girl living with her uncle in exile in Babylon. She attended a beauty pageant and was chosen to be King Xerxes' new queen. A while later she became aware of a genocide plot. She faced the dilemma of whether to speak up, knowing she faced death for such an act of insubordination. Her foster father challenged her directly, asking: 'And who knows but that you have come to royal position for such a time as this?' (Esther 4:14).

Our world is broken. Terrorism. Climate change. People trafficking. Slavery. Aids. Famine. They haunt our planet on a global scale. Who knows but that God has given you intellectual gifts so that you can be part of his solution to these problems? Who knows if God is raising you up to give your life to fight some of these evils? Will you follow Esther's example and risk all to stand up for those being exterminated by unjust regimes, by poverty and disease?

William Wilberforce is one example of a Christian in public life. He did not force the gospel on the nation through his powerful position as a member of the House of Commons. But instead, through rigorous argument, lobbying and persuasion he managed to convince Britain to ban a trade that was the backbone of our economy. It was his Christian conviction that all human beings are created equal that drove him to act. It took him and his team over twenty years of struggle to pass the bill that outlawed the transatlantic slave trade. What is less well known is that Wilberforce was also a founding member of the Church Mission Society and of the Royal Society for the Prevention of Cruelty to Animals. His love for God was demonstrated humbly by his love for neighbour and his care for creation. This made an impact in society. Here was a Christian with a sense of vocation.

Who will be the next William Wilberforce, Queen Esther, C. S. Lewis, Dorothy Sayers, Blaise Pascal, J. R. R. Tolkien? **We need Christians who make an impact through rigorous research, top-class thinking, godly lives, creativity, humility and hard work. Who knows but that you have come to university for such a time as this?**

WEEK 5: HOLINESS

UNIVERSITY CHALLENGE: WEEK 5

EXPRESSO CHALLENGE

Rate yourself out of 10 on the fruit of your spirit. Pick a character trait you think God would like you to work on specifically this week. Note down occasions when you have opportunities to exhibit these qualities.

	score	opportunity occasions
love		
joy		
peace		
patience		
kindness		
goodness		
faithfulness		
gentleness		
self-control		

EXTREME CHALLENGE

Start planning and raising funds now for a summer project during the long vacation. Check out the opportunities at www.christianvocations.org or at www.ifesinteraction.org.

OR

Adopt a child: see www.worldvision.org.uk.

OR

Become a supporter of Tearfund: http://youth.tearfund.org/students/.

EXPRESSION CHALLENGE

Kyle MacDonald started a trading experiment with one red paper clip on 12 July 2005. One year later, his fourteenth trade was a house.[10] Inspired by his story, try the red paper clip challenge for yourself to raise money for a development project.

Auction whatever you end up with on eBay and then write an article for the student newspaper and copy it to www.freshspace.org.

One night Homer Simpson meets God in a dream. Homer's God has a flowing white beard, sandals, yellow skin and five fingers. Homer's God agrees that Homer can worship God in any way that he likes. Homer's God agrees that Homer is not a bad person. Homer's God agrees that the people who get on Homer's nerves can be cursed with painful sores.

This episode of *The Simpsons*, 'Homer the heretic', is challenging because producer Matt Groening is pointing out how we often treat God in the Western church. Our God is like a friendly old man in the sky. Our God agrees with what we tell him. Our God is at our beck and call when we pray. Our God is on our side in any conflict. Our God enjoys whatever way that we choose to worship him.

How different this is from the God of the Bible. When prophets like John or Ezekiel catch only the tiniest glimpse of the shadow of God they fall down as if dead, overcome by his awesome majesty. Intimacy with God is an incredible privilege. But we often forget this as we become casual in our relationship with him. We need to recapture a bigger view of God. The author A. W. Tozer comments: 'The low view of God entertained almost universally among Christians is the cause of a hundred lesser evils.'[11]

God is described by John as light, in whom there is no darkness (1 John 1:5). Imagine something so bright, like the core of the sun, that darkness cannot exist near it. God's moral perfection is so complete that evil cannot exist in his presence; it is destroyed. Yet, by the grace of God we are invited into his family, to know and love him. But more than just being asked to join his family, we are commanded to take on his character.

Often the Bible tells us: 'Be holy, because I the Lord your God, am holy' (Leviticus 11:44–45; 19:2; 20:7; 1 Peter 1:16).

Never has a more difficult challenge been given to human beings. It's a bigger challenge than an Olympic sprinter telling us to 'be fast because I am fast' or Einstein telling us to 'be clever because I am clever'. We may feel overawed by the sporting or academic prowess of peers at university, but this is nothing in comparison to the moral standards that God is calling us to observe.

God tells us to be holy as he is holy. So our starting point can't be looking around at what others are doing or telling us to do. Our standard for morality must be God himself, who is set apart because of his moral perfection.

Holiness has often taken on a negative connotation. It is often perceived as a list of things we are forbidden to do. But when God's Holy

Spirit teaches us to be holy, the qualities he describes are far from negative:

But the fruit of the Spirit is love, joy, peace, patience, kindness, goodness, faithfulness, gentleness and self-control. Against such things there is no law. Those who belong to Christ Jesus have crucified the sinful nature with its passions and desires. Since we live by the Spirit, let us keep in step with the Spirit. (Galatians 5:22–25)

This view of the holy life is a positive and inspiring list of character qualities. In fact it is the kind of life that many non-Christians would like to have. It is the reason that Jesus is so attractive. Jesus perfectly demonstrates all of the character traits that are normal for those who live by the Spirit. To be holy is to be Christlike. The Holy Spirit will produce the fruit of the life of Christ in us, but we are also told to make sure we keep in step with him.

We are not on a short sprint to heaven, but a lifelong marathon. The Holy Spirit is like a champion runner who draws alongside us at the beginning of the race (John 14:15–27) and promises us that we will make it

to the end (Ephesians 1:13–14). He will help, challenge and encourage us. There will be times when we lean on him. There will be times when he pushes us forward. But the whole time we must keep in step with him.

> 'Your intimacy with God
> will affect your infuence for God.'
> (Tim Elmore)

Mae has been going to church all her life. She has been taught that Christians don't drink alcohol, so she's never been in a pub. She has been told that the media is a corrupting influence, so her family didn't own a TV. She has been told that rock music has satanic lyrics recorded backwards in them to try and hypnotize young people, so she only has praise CDs. Mae's first week at university was a tough one. It was as if she had landed on another planet. There was temptation everywhere: TV in the common room, all night drinking sessions, rock music blaring from every room. Mae ate breakfast before anyone else got up and cooked dinner while the others watched *Neighbours*. She was like a ghost on her corridor and her only oasis of sanity was the CU. She wrote this text up on her wall:

Dear friends, I urge you, as foreigners and exiles, to abstain from sinful desires, which war against your soul. (1 Peter 2:11)

Mina became a Christian in the summer holidays. She was beginning a film studies course and could recite all of Stanley Kubrick's scripts from memory. She played lead guitar in a new metal band that gigged regularly, raising money for the Sri Lankan orphanage her brother was involved in. Mina loved her first week at university and was the life and soul of the corridor. She joined Amnesty International and the Christian Union and spent her evenings drinking a pint or four. Her first CU meeting was a strange experience. She turned up with a cigarette, platform shoes and pink hair extensions, but felt very out of place, especially as nobody spoke to her. She would not go again. She also wrote a text from 1 Peter 2 on her wall:

Live such good lives among the pagans that, though they accuse you of doing wrong, they may see your good deeds and glorify God on the day he visits us. (1 Peter 2:12)

Both Mae and Mina are young Christians who need to grow in their understanding of holiness. Mae needs to hear Jesus' call to love the lost. She needs to have a less isolationist approach to holiness without losing her willingness to be set apart. Mina needs to hear Jesus' call to personal holiness without losing sight of her passion for culture and world transformation.

Godly living in the world was also something the Pharisees needed to learn. Jesus said:

Woe to you Pharisees, because you give God a tenth of your mint, rue and all other kinds of garden herbs, but you neglect justice and the love of God. You should have practiced the latter without leaving the former undone. (Luke 11:42)

Jesus is very critical of the holiness the Pharisees adopted. They followed the letter of the law. They were fastidious in their personal holiness, even going as far as giving a tenth of their herb gardens to God. But Jesus criticizes the Pharisees for having only an outward show of morality. He describes them as unmarked graves. Outwardly they look fine but internally they are ruled by greed, pride and arrogance (Luke 11:39, 44). The Pharisees' view of holiness was not deep or wide enough. They were concerned about personal holiness, but did not care for justice, or for integrity in national life. Not only did they not care for the needy, rather, they looked down on them and loaded them with religious rules.

Holiness for students needs to go beyond splitting hairs and beyond putting on airs. It needs to go beyond just having regular quiet times and being faithful in our church attendance. It needs to go beyond avoiding sex outside of marriage, watching our language, and knowing our drinking limits. We need to observe these while also pursuing the justice and the love of God (Amos 5:21–24).

The holiness of the Pharisees was careful that it did no wrong. But it ended up doing not much right. The medieval theologian Thomas Aquinas coined the phrase 'sins of commission and sins of omission'. There are things we are tempted to do wrong: blasphemy, theft, plagiarism, but there are also things that we fail to get right:

kindness, compassion and gentleness. The holy life should not lead to judgmental separation, but compassionate involvement in the lives of our non-Christian friends and in the places where we live, study and socialize.

> The one thing on which we can all agree, is that God is with the vulnerable and poor. God is in the slums and in the cardboard boxes where the poor play house. God is in the debris of wasted opportunity and lives, and God is with us if we are with them.
> (Bono)[12]

As we pursue God's agenda for both justice and love, we need to think seriously about our personal holiness. We want to avoid the narrow and shallow morality of the Pharisees and demonstrate the breadth and depth of God's love to a hurting world.

When we arrive at university all we have is a bootload of belongings. Unfortunately they are the first impression that we give to our new peers. Immediately, we feel measured up by the trainers on our feet, the car our parents drive off in, the iPod connected to our ears or the mobile phone in our pockets.

Financial pressure begins the moment we arrive at university, and it doesn't get any easier. We begin term feeling richer than we have ever felt and end it feeling poorer than we have ever felt. Coffee, phone credit and rent remind us daily of our new financial responsibilities.

Leo Tolstoy tells a story about a Russian business man who makes a deal with a Chechen landowner. The Russian can have as much land as he can run around from dusk until dawn. So as soon as the sun's first ray can be seen on the horizon, he throws off his jacket and runs for all he is worth. He runs all day, making his route wider to include more and more ground. As the sun begins to set, he makes an almighty effort to get back to the beginning, because if he doesn't the deal is off. As the last ray of the sun disappears, he sprints for the line. He makes it. But as he crosses the line he feels a pain in his chest and collapses dead on the ground. The story is entitled 'How much land does a man need?' The answer in the end is a plot of land 6 foot long and 6 foot deep.

It is hard in the pressure of university life to hear Jesus' words: 'Life does not consist in an abundance of possessions' (Luke 12:15).

This statement comes in the context of learning that we will all have to give an account of our lives before God. This accounting will include what we have done with the money God allowed us to look after for him.

Money is not evil. It is the LOVE of money that is the root of all kinds of evil (1 Timothy 6:10). And the love of money is not just a temptation for the rich. Poor students can love money too, causing them to be greedy for more, or to dive headlong into debt.

Rather than having an emotional relationship with money, we need to manage a practical relationship. This unfortunately means having a budget. Budgeting enables us to control our spending rather than have our spending control us.

The Bible has a lot to say about the dangers and temptations of money. Positively, it also has a lot to say about compassion, sacrifice, contentment and generosity (2 Corinthians 9:6–11).

GIVE GENEROUSLY

We have a generous God. We need to mirror him in all we do, and that includes our giving.

GIVE CHEERFULLY

We are saved by grace and that grace needs to spill over into every area of our lives. We can enjoy looking out for people who could benefit from a small, anonymous donation.

GIVE REGULARLY

We can prioritize our giving by writing those cheques at the beginning of term when we actually have something to give away.

GIVE STRATEGICALLY

This might be to our local church, to the CU, to world missions, to relief agencies and to needy people around us. Giving a lift, a cooked meal, or time may sometimes be more strategic than offering financial help.

GIVE SACRIFICIALLY

Jesus's parable of the widow's offering (Luke 21:1–4) tells us that God is not as concerned with how much we give as he is with how much we withhold. Giving sacrificially as a student can set in place a habit of godliness that can last for eternity.

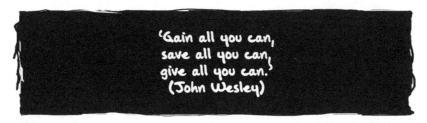

'Gain all you can,
save all you can,
give all you can.'
(John Wesley)

Ana had a tough decision to make. A man wanted to sleep with her and was making it very difficult for her to refuse. Everyone was doing it, but she wanted to take a stand. Why should she have to sleep with her professor in order to pass the year? In Bolivia this is a pretty common scenario. Ana was a Christian student and resisted her professor's overtures for several years, finally earning a pass without sleeping with him.[13]

The pressures facing students in the UK are different but call for the same resolve and courage.

Emma had a tough decision to make. Her boyfriend wanted to sleep with her, and yet she had taken a stand before university to wait until marriage. But at university it was harder. All her friends were doing it. She and her boyfriend were frequently alone in her bedroom and had all but decided to get married anyway. When her boyfriend began putting the pressure on, resistance seemed futile.

But among you there must not be even a hint of sexual immorality, or of any kind of impurity, or of greed, because these are improper for the Lord's people. (Ephesians 5:3)

For the set apart people of God, purity is an essential part of holiness. The Bible says that there must not be even a hint of sexual immorality. This means we have to think carefully about what we watch, wear and do, so that we can enjoy sex in the pure way it was designed to be enjoyed, while avoiding lust.

WATCH WHAT WE WATCH

With free internet access in our lockable private bedrooms, and 12% of all websites on the net offering porn,[14] many Christian students struggle with the temptation to look at inappropriate sites. Watching porn is harmful to ourselves as we begin to rate sexual activity above sexual intimacy within a loving relationship. It is also harmful to the actors, forced into porn via abduction, trafficking or prostitution. These vulnerable people are loved by God, and we can make a stand against this inhuman trade by refusing to support the industry. Ask friends to hold us accountable for our internet activity. Think about using Google's safety settings or downloading software such as x3watch from www.xxxchurch.com.

WATCH WHAT WE WEAR

Christians are not called to be fashion illiterates, but it is worth checking whether what we wear is sexually provocative. The if-you've-got-it-flaunt-it attitude of our culture is in direct opposition to God's attitude to clothes (1 Peter 3:2–4). We do not need to dress up, because we are made in the image of God. Nor do we need to dress down: God was the first person to design clothes and there is no reason to think that God did not do an excellent job of it.

WATCH WHAT WE DO

Our language, habits and flirtatiousness can often betray a cheapening attitude to sexuality. Late-night cuddles, or sleeping over on a friend's floor may cause unnecessary temptation. As we've seen, the Bible tells us that there must not be even a hint of sexual immorality. Why not adopt a transparent approach that puts us above reproach? Keeping doors open, having those determine-the-relationship talks, being honest with friends about our struggles, caring for our friends when they are hurt sexually, and courageously promoting sexual purity will make us, and more importantly the gospel, more attractive, not less.

The Bible also has a lot to say about the positive attributes of holiness that can help in our struggles against the many temptations in this area of sexuality. In fact, of the nine fruit of the Spirit, six can specifically help us stand out and be holy in this area: love, patience, kindness, faithfulness, gentleness and self-control.

Love that is selfless and unconditional puts other people and their needs above our own. Patience enables us to wait until God's timing to enjoy sex as he intended. Kindness thinks about how to help others around us, not put temptation in their paths.

Faithfulness refuses to sleep around for the sake of our life partner, even if we have not met him or her yet. Gentleness treats other people's bodies, hearts and feelings with respect.

Self-control teaches us to take charge of our sexuality by appropriate, godly behaviour.

Do you not know that the wicked will not inherit the kingdom of God? Do not be deceived: neither the sexually immoral nor idolaters nor adulterers nor male prostitutes nor practising homosexuals nor thieves nor the greedy nor drunkards nor slanderers nor swindlers will inherit the kingdom of God. And that is what some of you were. But you were washed, you were sanctified, you were justified in the name of the Lord Jesus Christ and by the Spirit of our God. (1 Corinthians 6:9–11)

This passage is very reassuring for those of us who feel we have completely messed up in the area of sexual purity. It shows us that sexual sins are not in a special 'most-disgraceful' category. They are mentioned alongside greed, slander and idolatry. Sexual sins are not unforgivable. Many of Paul's readers had found forgiveness and cleansing. And it shows us that it's not too late. If necessary, ask someone in your local church to provide you with some counselling help.

'With great power comes great responsibility.' (Spiderman)[15]

Students throughout history have wielded incredible political power. The students of Tiananmen Square in 1989 drew the world's attention to the injustices of Chinese communism. Student demonstrations in Albania were decisive in bringing a bloodless end to communism. Students in the Ukraine were instrumental in the Orange Revolution which challenged corrupt elections, and Christian students were there right in the middle of it all, running a prayer tent, offering hot drinks and warm clothes.

We may often feel powerless, but as students we actually wield quite an influence in the university. We bring in the fees for the courses and our feedback on tutors may affect their careers. The banks are keen to sign us up, IT companies want our loyalty, career fairs are after our futures, our housemates want our respect and approval.

How we acknowledge and use that power is significant for us as Christians as it will makes us stand out from the world around us.

James and John decided that being students of Jesus was becoming a promising career prospect. They asked for promotion to be his right- and left-hand men: one of them on either side of Jesus when his power over the universe was revealed. When the other disciples heard about this request they were upset. Jesus steps in:

You know that those who are regarded as rulers of the Gentiles lord it over them, and their high officials exercise authority over them. Not so with you. Instead, whoever wants to become great among you must be your servant, and whoever wants to be first must be slave of all. For even the Son of Man did not come to be served, but to serve, and to give his life as a ransom for many. (Mark 10:42–45)

Jesus is the most powerful being in the universe. Yet when he is starving after a forty-day fast, he refuses to turn stones into bread. When the crowds hurl insults at him he does not retaliate. When the soldiers crucify him he refuses to call down angels to protect him.

But when there are hungry people in the wilderness, Jesus turns five loaves into enough food for 5,000 to eat. When the Pharisees are sneering at an immoral woman who is washing Jesus' feet with her hair, he defends her. When the wind is frightening his disciples, he exercises his authority and the storm is stilled.

Jesus refuses to use his power for his own benefit, but does all in his power for the benefit of others. This is the model of a holy use of power. Let's see how this works in a university setting.

SOCIAL POWER

Christians have a bad reputation for being judgmental. But the Bible teaches that in Christ there is genuine equality: no longer slave and free, Jew or Gentile, male or female. We need to make sure that we are using our social power to demonstrate this equality: between men and women, between popular and unpopular students, between home and international students, and between those of different faiths.

In Rwanda it was Christian students who were often killed first in the genocide because they had worked hard to promote the equality of Hutu and Tutsi students. Jesus was persecuted for his socializing with women, prostitutes and sinners. It is not an easy calling, but a holy use of power includes using our social influence so that the excluded are welcomed and the outcasts accepted.

CONSUMER POWER

How we spend our money is a way of using our economic power to help or hinder God's agenda in the world. Buying fairly-traded goods is a way of enforcing the biblical principle that workers are worth their wages. We can encourage the CU, our department and our sports clubs to think ethically about their purchases at events. We have the option of putting our money into an ethical bank account. We can also think about the environmental impact of our consumer choices, showing that we care about God's planet. Cycling to college or using the bus is a simple way that we can show positive holiness.

POLITICAL POWER

Student politics is open to all students and offers a good introduction to politics generally. We should think about how we use our vote, what we campaign for and how we use our voice in the student newspaper, campus radio or in the hustings meetings.

INTELLECTUAL POWER

Society naturally has layers of people from different educational backgrounds. At university we get used to dealing only with one tier. But this makes us susceptible to becoming elitist when we leave. We should think about keeping our feet on the ground across the spectrum. This can happen at a local church, or through deliberately taking part in other community projects.

Albanian students in the 1990s had some tough decisions to make. Should they finish their courses and become underpaid medics in corrupt hospital systems, or should they earn twice as much in Italy as waiters? Should they freeze to death in their draughty dorms with broken windows and one-bar electric heaters – or should they wire their iron bed frames to the mains so that they glowed red and gave off enough heat to keep warm? Should they have beans for supper again, or hunt down a tortoise to boost the nutritional content of the meal? I spent many hours with these students, laughing with them at the creative lengths they would go to in order to endure the harsh conditions at university.

It is to the poor that Jesus speaks when he offers these words of comfort:

So do not worry, saying, 'What shall we eat?' or 'What shall we drink?' or 'What shall we wear?' For the pagans run after all these things, and your heavenly Father knows that you need them. But seek first his kingdom and his righteousness, and all these things will be given to you as well. *Therefore do not worry about tomorrow, for tomorrow will worry about itself. Each day has enough trouble of its own.* (Matthew 6:31–34)

Our take on these verses does not revolve around wondering where our next meal will come from, or whether we have enough clothes to keep us warm enough to survive the cold nights. 'What shall we eat?' for us means tuna pasta bake or chicken casserole, Jamie Oliver or Gordon Ramsay. 'What shall we wear?' for us means Bench or Gap, bootleg or slim-fit.

Jesus' words still ring true. Seek first God's agenda. Let the pagans spend their lives focused on the concerns of fashion and cuisine.

I once saw a cartoon which showed a herd of lemmings running off a cliff. One of the lemmings stood out. He was running off the cliff too but he wore a life jacket and a knowing smile. Many Christians are like this lemming. We follow the crowd with our life goals and personal ambitions. We chase the same things: well-paid jobs, flashy gadgets, fast cars, large houses. But we smile, knowing that we have the spiritual life jacket or a get-out-of-hell-free card. Jesus tells us that we are actually called to run in the opposite direction – to seek God's kingdom, God's agenda in the world.

If we checked how each of our decisions fits in with God's agenda, we might see a dramatic shift in the way we live. It would affect how we choose to spend our time and money, and the friendships and lifestyle we adopt. It would affect our priorities and our plans. But that does not mean that life would be any easier!

It's Wednesday night and the guys in Rafael's volleyball team are going to a local club in town. Doors open at 11 pm and they're not going to get home before 4 am. Rafael is just beginning to make friends with the guys on the squad. He doesn't want to look like a Christian spoilsport, but he knows he has to get up for his 9 am to 4 pm lab the next day. He also knows they are going to get hammered and pull girls. Should he go?

It could give Rafael the chance to deepen the friendships he is making. It could bring genuine opportunities to help people out of the difficult situations they often get into when they are drunk. He would enjoy the dancing and music. He would have the opportunity to dispel the myth that Christians are boring. He would show that it is possible to go to a club and not be ruled by the values that normally operate there.

Not going on the trip would give Rafael the chance to get the rest he needs and not turn up at the lab like a sleep-deprived zombie, a real liability for his lab partner. He would not be short tempered and non-communicative. He would be awake enough to learn the skills he needs for his calling as a scientist. Rafael would not have to worry about whether or not he would be able to resist the temptation of joining in the drinking and flirting. By taking a stand early on in the friendships, he could save himself difficulties further down the road.

I wish decision-making was clear cut. I do not know the right answer for Rafael. I wish there was a simple formula. It is true that sometimes God guides us very specifically. The book of Acts tells us that God spoke directly to Paul in a dream to make sure he went to Macedonia, but at other times Paul had to make decisions based on general biblical principles, counsel from friends, common sense and good planning. The same is true for us. Sometimes God speaks to us directly, but at other times he leaves us to make wise decisions.

This example shows that God could be honoured, whichever path Rafael takes. Making wise decisions is part of maturing as a Christian. In the end, Rafael can pray, ask for advice from other Christians, be honest with his volleyball friends about his dilemma, and trust God for whichever path he chooses. In the end, our call is to seek first God's kingdom and make the best decisions we can.

Sadly, it's an all-too-common story. Chris begins his time at university with great hopes. He plans to get stuck in and make an impact for Christ. He nails his colours to the mast as a Christian early on and confidently lets people know he is saving sex for marriage. But a few weeks later he gets drunk and sleeps with one of the girls from his corridor. Next morning everyone knows. Chris feels he has let himself and God down. He is embarrassed every time he leaves his room and can't face going to CU. He bunks lectures and is torn between drowning his sorrows in the bar and dropping out of university altogether.

This book has set some high standards and issued some strong challenges. Jesus really does call us to radical discipleship at university. However, as the Lord of the fresh start, Jesus also offers a radically generous helping of grace.

One of the best loved stories in the Bible is God's dealing with a shepherd boy called David. It's a classic rags-to-riches story. From baby brother tending sheep, to Israel's poster boy for giant-killing, to popular king of the nation. He becomes known throughout the ancient world for his victories in God's name. But one day he bunks his duty as commander-in-chief and drools over a beautiful woman bathing next door. He has a choice to turn his eyes away, but he lets them linger, and temptation turns to sin. Next thing we know he is sleeping with this married beauty, a baby is on the way and David has conspired to murder her husband (2 Samuel 11).

He has gone far too far. Surely a fresh start is out of the question. It takes a brave prophet to challenge a king who had already committed one murder. But Nathan valiantly and tactfully confronts David. With great turmoil of mind, David pens another one of those psalms that speak straight from the heart.

The words he writes in Psalm 51 can become a prayer for anyone who feels a failure. The verses are like steps for us to follow to find our way home.

STEP 1: ASK FOR MERCY

Have mercy on me, O God,
    according to your unfailing love;
according to your great compassion
    blot out my transgressions.
Wash away all my iniquity
    and cleanse me from my sin.
(verses 1–2)

David does not ask God to forgive him because he is a good person deep down, because he has done some great things for God, or because he promises never to do it again. David asks for mercy because he knows he has blown it and he knows of God's unfailing love and great compassion. Step one is to own up to the God who does not treat us as our sins deserve.

STEP 2: ASK GOD TO CLEAN YOU

Cleanse me with hyssop, and I shall be clean;
*   wash me, and I will be whiter than snow.*
(verse 7)

Sin stains us and makes us feel dirty. No matter how hard we scrub we can't clean ourselves up. David believes that only God can give him a clean conscience. This is the fresh start we long for, and it is available when we take step 2 and ask God for it.

STEP 3: ASK GOD TO CHANGE YOUR HEART

Create in me a pure heart, O God,
*   and renew a steadfast spirit within me.*
(verse 10)

David doesn't just want a reputation makeover. He wants to be made pure from the inside out. He wants spiritual renewal to enable him to resist temptation next time round. This isn't just feeling bad about getting caught. This is step 3: a heart's cry to be pure.

STEP 4: EXPECT GOD TO TURN IT TO GOOD

Then I will teach transgressors your ways,
and sinners will turn back to you.
(verse 13)

Here is truly one sinful beggar telling another where to find forgiveness. David wants to be right with God so he can serve God again. God's grace is so big that it can far overshadow our sin before a watching world. Step 4 involves watching in amazement as God restores us and reuses us.

David has to face serious consequences for his sin: a lost baby, a broken heart and public humiliation. But God also gives David genuine restoration and a renewed spiritual passion. David had many years of faithful and fruitful service to God after his moral collapse.

The Bible reassures us that, if we come to God with a broken spirit and a contrite heart, this fresh start comes with his forgiveness. If we have been going through the motions of the Christian faith because that is what has been expected of us, this fresh start is a chance to get real with God. If we have got stuck in a rut, it is an opportunity to blaze a new trail. If we have watched Christians from the outside, but never really understood what all the fuss was about, this fresh start offers us a chance to take an adult look at putting Jesus first in our life.

An artist stands before a blank canvas. It is not just a piece of paper, it is a potential masterpiece. A new word document on the desktop has the potential to be the next bestselling novel. A fresh start, whether in freshers' week or finals week is an exciting gift from God and a chance for him to do something extraordinary with our lives.

NOTES

1. Dietrich Bonhoeffer, *Cost of Discipleship* (SCM, 1996), p. 79.
2. Tearfund, *Churchgoing in the UK*, 2007.
3. Cited in a speech by Robert Boucher, vice-chancellor of Sheffield University and chairman of Universities UK's international strategy group, 24 May 2005 (<http://education.guardian.co.uk/students/overseasstudents/story/0,12743,1491188,00.html>).
4. C. S. Lewis, 'Learning in war-time', in *Weight of Glory: and Other Addresses* (Zondervan, 2001).
5. James D. Bratt, *Abraham Kuyper: A Centennial Reader* (Eerdmans, 2002), p. 488.
6. See <http://www.stopthetraffik.org> and <http://www.humantrafficking.org> for more information.
7. Morpheus in *The Matrix* (Warner Bros., 1999).
8. Episode 6, <http://www.catalystspace.com>.
9. T. R. Glover, *The Jesus of History* (Indypublish, 2005).
10. Read about it at <http://oneredpaperclip.blogspot.com>.
11. A. W. Tozer, *Knowledge of the Holy* (OM Publishing, 1991), p. 7.
12. Bono, *On the Move* (Thomas Nelson, 2007).
13. Lindsay Brown, *Shine Like Stars* (IVP, 2006), p. 107.
14. Source <http://xxxchurch.com>.
15. The tagline of the film (Sony Pictures, 2002).